PRIVATE VIOLENCE
AND PUBLIC POLICY

PRIVATE VIOLENCE AND PUBLIC POLICY

The needs of battered women and the response of the public services

Edited by Jan Pahl

ROUTLEDGE & KEGAN PAUL
London, Boston, Melbourne and Henley

First published in 1985
by Routledge & Kegan Paul plc

14 Leicester Square, London WC2H 7PH, England

9 Park Street, Boston, Mass. 02108, USA

464 St Kilda Road, Melbourne,
Victoria 3004, Australia and

Broadway House, Newtown Road,
Henley-on-Thames, Oxon RG9 1EN, England

Set in Melior 10/12 pt.
by Columns of Reading
and printed in Great Britain
by St Edmundsbury Press Ltd,
Bury St Edmunds, Suffolk

Library of Congress Cataloging in Publication Data

Private violence and public policy.
Bibliography: p.
Includes index.
1. Abused wives—England—Longitudinal studies.
2. Abused wives—Services for—England. 3. Family policy
—England. I. Pahl, J. M.
HV6626.P74 1985   362.8'3   84-15952

ISBN 0-7100-9992-4 (pbk.)

Contents

Editor's acknowledgments

The Department of Health and Social Security funded not only my own study but also the conference at which all the other work described in this book was presented: I should like to thank Phoebe Hall, in particular, for her friendly and constructive support. My own study, and the conference, took place at the University of Kent at Canterbury. I am grateful to the university and especially to those members of the Health Services Research Unit and the Board of Studies in Social Policy and Administration who have taken an interest in my work. In particular, I should like to thank Ray Pahl for his support, both collegial and domestic. I am grateful to all whose secretarial skills went into preparing this book, but especially to Barbara Holland and Shirley Woodward, who typed the final version with speed and accuracy. This is also the place at which to emphasise that the views expressed in this book are those of the authors, and do not necessarily represent the views of the funding bodies. Finally, my warmest thanks go to all the women who participated in my study: I hope that the results will justify the kindness they showed me and the trust they placed in me.

Chapter one

Introduction

This book had its origins in a conference which was funded by the Department of Health and Social Security and which took place at the University of Kent at Canterbury in September 1981. The conference brought together several very different groups of people: researchers who had been investigating different aspects of wife abuse, practitioners who met battered women in the course of their work, and policy makers with responsibility for a wide range of welfare services. The practitioners included social workers, housing managers, doctors, nurses, health visitors, solicitors, policemen and policewomen, marriage guidance counsellors and workers in refuges and in advice centres. The participants also included a number of women who had had personal experience of being battered. The conference was such a success that it seemed important that the knowledge and understanding which it generated should be made available to a wider audience. This book is the result. It is aimed not only at those working in the professions mentioned above, but also at people training for those professions, at students in the relevant social science disciplines, and at all those who have an interest in the changing nature of family life.

The book falls into three parts. The aim of the first part is to give readers a better understanding of the problem of wife abuse, by looking in some detail at the experiences of one group of women. This part of the book is based on the editor's own study, which was carried out at a women's refuge in the south-east of England. This study followed the lives of forty-two women and their 124 children over a period of three years in the late 1970s. All but one of the women had husbands who had been violent towards them, and all had left home with their children to find shelter in a women's refuge. The women were interviewed at the refuge and then re-interviewed about two years later after they had left it. This was a unique study in that it investigated marital breakdown, not retrospectively and after it had ended in divorce or separation, but as it was experienced by a group of women during the time when they were considering whether the breakdown should be permanent or temporary.

The second part of the book draws together a number of papers which were presented at the conference. Most of these papers presented the findings of specific research projects. The work covered in these projects ranged far more widely than the material presented at the conference (see Binney, Harkell and Nixon, 1980a and 1981; Borkowski, Murch and Walker, 1983; Dawson and Faragher, 1977; Delamont and Ellis, 1979; Dobash and Dobash, 1979 and 1980; Evason, 1982; Frankenberg *et al.*, 1980; Leonard and McLeod, 1980; Murch, 1981; Pahl, 1978 and 1981). However, for the purposes of the conference speakers were asked to direct their papers to the question of how practitioners might give more effective and appropriate help to battered women. The hope was that the conference would foster better practice in a field of work which is often seen as posing great difficulties.

The third part of the book represents the contribution of those who participated in the conference, not as researchers but as people whose work brings them into contact with family violence. The design of the conference reflected the hope that it would not be a one-way event, in which researchers addressed a passive audience, but that it would encourage a two-way flow of ideas between researchers and practitioners. To this end a substantial amount of time was given to small discussion groups, each of which reported back to the conference as a whole at the end of the three days. Part III of this book draws on the reports of the discussion groups: it aims to offer some constructive recommendations for the future, both in terms of better practice and in terms of broader social and economic policy changes.

In many ways, then, this is a very practical book, presenting the results of a series of studies which were focused on a particular problem in family life. Those who are familiar with this topic may assume that a book about wife abuse is concerned with a marginal and insignificant, if horrific, aspect of family life. However, closer consideration of the problem of wife abuse shows that the problem raises fundamental theoretical issues about the nature of family life which have a very broad relevance.

One such broad theoretical issue concerns the relationship between the public and the private. As we shall see, this issue has exercised the minds of philosophers over the centuries, but it is perhaps of greater significance now than at any time in the past. The growth of the welfare state and the increased intervention of the state into family life have been paralleled by a growth in concern for the privacy of the home and for the rights of the private individual. This issue is raised in a particularly acute form in the problem of wife abuse. We shall argue in this book that the violence which husbands inflict on their wives is different from other sorts of violence in that it normally takes place in a particular location and within a particular set of social relations. It follows that it is impossible to understand the nature of wife abuse without taking account of the fact, firstly, that it most often occurs within private homes, and secondly, that it occurs between two people who are bound together by marriage or a marriage-like relationship.

Wife abuse is an emotive topic, not just because the injuries which women receive provoke feelings of shock and pity, but also because it takes place in a setting which we perceive as being a safe haven in a heartless world and within a relationship which for many people is a source of happiness and security. We are shocked at the injuries, but we are also shocked that such things could occur in a domestic setting, between two people who have promised to love and cherish each other. The discrepancy between the violence and the setting within which it takes place both makes it harder to understand the problem and also makes it harder to help those who are the victims. We shall return to the question of helping wives who are the victims of violence in Part II of this book. However, before discussing the more theoretical issue of the distinction between the public and the private, let us first consider, in very broad factual terms, what is known about the problem of wife abuse.

What do we mean by violence against wives?

It is important to recognise that violence can take many forms and that it includes both physical and mental assault. The evidence from many studies is that the violence experienced by wives is both prolonged and severe. In my own study 62 per cent of the women had been subjected to violence for three or more years, and the injuries which they had suffered ranged from cuts and bruises, through broken bones and damaged eyesight, to a ruptured spleen, stab wounds and a fractured skull. The findings of this small study are confirmed by the results of a much larger study, undertaken at the same time in all the refuges of England and Wales, by Binney, Harkell and Nixon. This larger study found that 73 per cent of women in refuges had put up with violence for three or more years. Thirty per cent of the women who were interviewed in this study had suffered life-threatening attacks or had been hospitalised for serious injuries such as having bones broken. The rest of the sample had experienced assaults which included being kicked, pushed into fires or through glass, being thrown against walls or down stairs, being punched and having hair pulled out. Sixty-eight per cent said that mental cruelty was one of the reasons why they left home (Binney, Harkell and Nixon, 1981). Dobash and Dobash found that the women they interviewed in Scottish refuges had experienced a variety of different forms of violence. This violence ranged from a single slap, usually experienced early in the marriage, to an attack involving kicking, punching and choking; on occasions the men would use belts, bottles or weapons. The most typical attack involved punches to the face and/or body, and kicks (Dobash and Dobash, 1980, 106). One definition of the problem is that 'a battered wife is a wife or cohabitee who has suffered persistent or serious physical assault at the hands of her partner' (Marsden, 1978); however, to this definition must be added the comment of many women, that 'the mental battering was worse than the physical battering'.

There is some dispute about whether we should use the words 'battered women' or 'battered wives'. The former term is a reminder that women can be battered by their co-habitees and ex-husbands as well as by their spouse. The latter term is a reminder that, whatever the legal status of the couple, the violence takes place in a marriage-like situation. That is to say that the couple have children in common, that they share a home or have shared a home, and that the woman is likely to be financially dependent on the man.

What is more significant is that we use the term 'battered wives' rather than 'violent husbands'. It is rather as though the problem of international terrorists hijacking aeroplanes was described as 'the problem of hostages'! The effect of this re-naming of the problem is to shift attention from the instigators of the violence to its victims, and the shift tends to make it easy to blame the victim for the problem and to encourage a search for solutions among the victims rather than among the violent partners. This misnaming is probably no accident. A great many people hold to the view that battered women are somehow responsible for what has happened to them, and this view is expressed in such statements as 'the woman must have done something to deserve it' or 'women must enjoy it really, otherwise surely they would leave'. The tragedy is that battered women themselves share the popularly held assumption that they are to blame for what is happening; they continue to blame themselves and to feel guilty about the violence, and this is one reason why they do not leave but continue to endure the violence.

The evidence from my own study is that, of the women who remarried between the two interviews, not one was being abused in her new relationship. On the other hand, every refuge has stories about individual men, each one of whom, when one woman has finally obtained a divorce from him on the grounds of cruelty, marries again and starts to batter yet another woman. It is the men who are violence-prone and not the women. When we are considering short-term help for battered women, in the form of legislative changes, better services or more refuges, then it makes sense to talk of the problem of battered women. But when we consider more long-term fundamental solutions we should remember that the problem is more accurately described as the problem of violent husbands.

What proportion of all violence takes the form of violence against wives? There are considerable difficulties in answering this question since so much violence, both inside and outside the home, goes unrecorded. The best sources of evidence are

Introduction

police records, but even these pose problems, especially in the case of private crimes such as wife assault and rape, where the victims are often reluctant to report the crime because of feelings of guilt, shame and loyalty. There is considerable 'shrinkage': crimes may occur but may not be reported to the police; they may be reported but not recorded. And then, of course, more 'shrinkage' occurs between the crime being recorded and the case coming to court.

However, there does seem to be agreement between a number of different sources which suggest that assault of wives by their husbands is by far the most common form of family violence. Important evidence comes from the study of Dobash and Dobash, who analysed the police records of Edinburgh and Glasgow. Their findings are presented in Table 1.1. This table shows that the most common form of violence

Table 1.1: Offences involving violence reported to selected police departments in Edinburgh and Glasgow in 1974

Offence	Total number of offences	Percentage of offences
Violent: Family		
Wife assault	776	24.14
Alleged wife assault	32	1.00
Husband assault	13	0.40
Child assault	110	3.42
Parent assault	70	2.18
Sibling assault	50	1.56
	(1051)	(32.70)
Violent: Non-family		
Male against male	1196	37.20
Male against female	292	9.08
Male against police	452	14.06
Female against female	142	4.42
Female against male	53	1.65
Female against police	29	0.90
	(2164)	(67.31)
Total	3215	100.00

Source: Dobash and Dobash (1980)

is that which takes place between unrelated males, which makes up 37 per cent of all recorded violent incidents. The second most common form of violence is wife assault, which makes up 25 per cent of all recorded violent crime. By comparison, the other forms of violence between family members, such as assault on husbands, on children, elderly parents and siblings, are relatively insignificant. When one thinks of the attention which is directed towards street violence, concern with assault on wives seems long overdue. What we are discussing in this book represents one-quarter of all violent crime. (See also McClintock, 1963; Chester and Streather, 1972).

We must remember, however, the differential rates of both the reporting and the recording of crimes of violence. It is unlikely that assault on a policeman will go unrecorded, and so we can consider the recorded total of these offences as a reasonably accurate reflection of the occurrence of assaults. On the other hand, assaults on wives and on children are very much less likely to end up as entries in police records and so the recorded totals must be seen as under estimates of the true extent of these problems. After careful and detailed interviews with large numbers of abused wives, the Dobashes concluded that only about 2 per cent of all such assaults are ever reported to the police (Dobash and Dobash, 1980, 164).

One important measure of the extent of wife abuse is the dramatic proliferation of refuges in Britain over the past few years. From the setting up of the first refuge for battered women in Chiswick in 1971, the number has grown so that by 1981 there were about 200 refuges scattered across the country. The majority of these refuges are affiliated to the Women's Aid Federations of England, Scotland, Wales and Northern Ireland. They provide safe accommodation for women and their children, advice of whatever sort the woman requires and support for as long as she needs it. The fact that most refuges are usually extremely overcrowded suggests that the women who go to them represent the desperate tip of a very large iceberg. The Women's Aid Federation calculate that in any one year about 12,000 women and 21,000 children will use refuge accommodation, and that at any one time about 1,000 women and 1,700 children will be living in refuges (Women's Aid Federation, 1980a). However, provision of refuges is still very far from the level recommended by the Select Committee on Violence in Marriage which proposed that 'One family place per 10,000 of the population should be the initial target' (Select Committee Report, 1975, xxvi).

Another question concerns the extent of violence in family life and within marriage. A difficulty here is that so little is known about the extent of violence in ordinary families. Most of our knowledge about wife abuse comes from the accounts of wives who have gone to refuges, or from studies of divorcing couples. In both instances it seems likely that a greater proportion of middle-class, as opposed to working-class violence, goes unreported.

The only large study to have investigated violence in the general population was carried out in the United States by Straus, Gelles and Steinmetz. The first paragraph reads:

> Drive down any street in America. More than one household in six has been the scene of a spouse striking his or her partner last year. Three American households in five (which have children living at home) have reverberated with the sounds of parents hitting their children. Where there is more than one child in the home, three in five are the scenes of violence between siblings. Overall, every other house in America is the scene of family violence at least once a year (Straus, Gelles and Steinmetz, 1980).

This study showed that, while in any one year violence occurs in 16 per cent of American marriages, if the entire marriage period is considered, violence has occurred in 28 per cent of American marriages. Though wives are violent as well as husbands, the damage inflicted by husbands is more dangerous, causes more harm, and is more frequently inflicted.

In Britain, Hanmer's study of community violence to women showed that 59 per cent of the women interviewed had experienced violent or threatening attacks during the previous year, 21 per cent of these at home (Hanmer, 1983). What about violence within marriage? Drawing together such evidence as there is, Marsden suggested that serious violence takes place in up to 5 per cent of British marriages and less serious violence in about another 1 per cent (Marsden, 1978). These percentages are, however, extremely tentative and perhaps the most realistic answer to our question was given by the Select Committee Report:

> Despite our efforts, we are unable to give any estimates of what the likely numbers are; several witnesses talked to us in terms of the tip of an iceberg and this seems to us to be correct. Most witnesses agreed, and this is almost certainly correct, that all strata of society are involved, although the better off are perhaps less likely to seek outside help. (Select Committee, 1975)

Why does violence occur?

Broadly speaking, there are two approaches to causal analysis of this problem. The first approach locates the problem within the individuals concerned and seeks to explain the violence in terms of deviant or pathological personalities. The work of Faulk, for example, which was concerned with men who had been convicted of wife abuse, showed that a majority of them could be classified as being mentally ill in one way or another (Faulk, 1974). However, other studies have not so far confirmed this finding, which was, of course, carried out with an unusual group in that all the men had actually been convicted of assault. Several researchers have found a link between violence and excessive consumption of alcohol. In my own study 52 per cent of the women said that their husbands often drank to excess, and this is similar to the proportions recorded by Gelles (1974) and Gayford (1975). However, it has been suggested that drunkenness should be seen not as a 'cause' of violence but as a condition which co-exists with it. Thus men who wish to carry out a violent act may become intoxicated in order to have the courage to perform the act. After violence has occurred both the man and his wife may excuse his behaviour on the grounds that since he had been drunk he could not be held responsible for what had happened.

Violent personalities are also seen as being a consequence of childhood experiences. The study carried out by Straus, Gelles and Steinmetz showed that people who grew up in violent homes were more likely to use violence than those who had not. Thus one in ten of husbands who grew up in violent families were wife beaters in the sense of serious assault, and this is over three times the rate for husbands who did not grow up in such homes. However, the researchers point out that it would be a mistake to put too great a burden on what is learned in the family. To see this one needs only to look at the violence rates for children of non-violent parents. These rates show that a considerable amount of violence is perpetrated by people whose parents were not violent to them and not violent to each other. The family may be a training ground for violence, but for a fuller explanation we have to look to the wider society (Straus, Gelles and Steinmetz, 1980). There is now a considerable number of studies which put forward a variety of causal explanations of wife abuse. For more extended discussion of these see especially Freeman (1979), Hanmer (1978) and Martin (1978). In general it can be said that causal analyses of the problem are divided between the individual and the social-structural approach.

The second approach locates the problem in a broader social-structural context and focuses, not narrowly upon the individual, but upon the whole social situation within which the violence takes place. Here explanation is in terms of social context rather than in terms of individuals, and here new light can be thrown upon the behaviour of individuals. For example, this explanation would look beyond the link between drunkenness and battering to consider the way in which some cultures see both phenomena as symptoms of masculinity and male dominance. The social-structural explanation would, similarly, look beyond the fact that a drunken man committed an assault, to recognise that if he assaults a policeman he is likely to be prosecuted, while if he assaults his wife it is likely to be labelled a 'domestic dispute' for which police intervention is kept to a minimum. And this explanation would see the fact that some women return again and again to their violent husbands, not as a result of some sort of sado-masochism, but as a consequence of the inadequate help given to battered women and the hardships experienced by women who are trying to bring up children by themselves.

The legitimisation of violence by the wider society is an important part of this broader structural approach. This legitimisation is woven into a culture at every level, from the level of popular saying to the level of legislation. An important part of this legitimisation is the denial that wife abuse takes place, or the assertion that its occurrence is rare and is confined to unusual or deviant couples. In recent years, however, evidence has accumulated to confirm that violence against wives occurs in many very different societies, and at all social levels. It would be incorrect to see violence as confined to Britain and to the working class within Britain. Throughout this book reference is made to British and American studies. However, it is important to note the existence of studies of wife abuse in Germany (Hagemann-White, 1981), Israel (Saunders, 1982), the Mediterranean (Loizos, 1978), Amazonia (Chagnon, 1968) and Mexico (Roldan, 1982), and the existence of refuges or shelters for battered women in Britain, the United States, Holland, West Germany, Switzerland, Belgium, Canada, France, Australia, New Zealand and Israel (Dobash and Dobash, 1980). Schlegel rated forty-five societies and showed that three-quarters of them permitted husbands to be aggressive towards their wives (Schlegel, 1972).

Just as wife abuse takes place in the majority of societies, so it has been condoned throughout most of history. Historically the tradition of accepting wife assault is longer than the tradition of deploring it. Until the nineteenth century British law gave to husbands the right to beat their wives for what was called 'lawful correction', and it was only excessive beating that was frowned upon. The law reflected and upheld a hierarchical and patriarchal family structure. This tradition was summarised by Blackstone in the late eighteenth century as follows:

> The husband also might give his wife moderate correc-
> tion. For as he is to answer for her misbehaviour the law
> thought it reasonable to entrust him with this power of
> restraining her, by domestic chastisement in the same
> moderation that a man is allowed to correct his servant
> or children. (Blackstone, 1966, vol. 1, 432)

A precedent was set by Judge Buller in 1782 when he declared that legally a husband could beat his wife so long as he did not use a stick thicker than his thumb. This legal right was not finally removed until 1891 (R. v. Jackson). Dickens reflected both contemporary awareness of wife beating in, for example, the savage attack which Bill Sykes makes on Nancy in *Oliver Twist*, and also the nineteenth century's casual acceptance of it: thus he makes Sam Weller, in *Pickwick Papers*, talk about what he calls 'the amiable weakness of wife beating'. There is now a substantial literature on the ways in which wife abuse has been practised, condoned and indeed approved of throughout recorded history (see especially Dobash and Dobash, 1980; May, 1978; Sutton, 1979; Tomes, 1978). The casual acceptance of wife beating is still with us today. A new graffiti was chalked up in the summer of 1981 in the shelter at Bekesbourne, a small railway station among the orchards and hopfields between Canterbury and Dover. The graffiti took the form of a question and an answer:

> Q. *Which is the odd one out? Mat, egg, wife, sex?*
> A. Sex. Because you can beat a mat, an egg and a wife, but you can't beat sex.

Thus is wife beating culturally legitimated and prolonged.

Any explanation of wife assault needs to be located in the broader social context, and in particular in the context of the structural and ideological forces which shape the relationships between men and women both within marriage and in the wider society. Straus summed up the conclusions of the recent large-scale survey of violence in American families by saying, 'the causes of wife-beating are to be found in the very structure of American society and its family system' (Straus, 1978, 41; see also Breines and Gordon, 1983).

A very careful and detailed British study of wife beating was that carried out by Dobash and Dobash in Scotland. In that study the assaults which the women had endured were investigated not as isolated incidents, but as part of the whole relationship between the couple, as it had developed from courtship to marriage to child bearing and rearing. The Dobashes concluded:

> We propose that the correct interpretation of violence between husbands and wives conceptualises such violence as the extension of the domination and control of husbands over wives. This control is historically and socially constructed. The beginning of an adequate

analysis of violence between husbands and wives is the consideration of the history of the family, of the status of women therein, and of violence directed against them. This analysis will substantiate our claim that violence in the family should be understood primarily as coercive control. (Dobash and Dobash, 1980, 15)

Clearly it is important, not simply to describe the violence inflicted by one individual on another, but to extend the analysis to take into account the social and economic context within which the violence takes place. The literature on wife abuse has pointed to a number of different aspects of marriage and family life as being conducive to the occurrence of violence. One aspect which has not so far received much attention, however, is the fact that the violence takes place in the privacy of the family home and within what is defined as the most private of all relationships. It is to this aspect of the problem that we now turn.

Public and private

The dichotomy between public and private must be of concern to those who seek to understand the roots of violence against wives and to those who want to help the victims of violence in the home. In a culture which, both explicitly and implicitly, assumes fundamental linkages between such concepts as 'woman', 'wife', 'family', 'home' and 'private', it is no accident that violence against a woman, perpetuated by her husband within their family home, is somehow seen as a different sort of crime from violence against a stranger in a public place. We can see these linkages exemplified in many different statements which have been made on the subject, most especially in the justifications for non-intervention given both by violent husbands, and also by people who might well have intervened had the violence occurred between strangers in a public place. The two following examples both come from the Select Committee Report on *Violence in Marriage*. The first is an extract from the evidence presented by the Association of Chief Police Officers:

Introduction

It is important to keep 'wife battering' in its correct perspective and realise that this loose term is applied to incidents ranging from a very minor domestic fracas where no Police action is really justified, to the more serious incidents of assaults occasioning grievous bodily harm and unlawful woundings. Whilst such problems take up considerable Police time during say, 12 months, in the majority of cases the role of the Police is a negative one. We are, after all, dealing with persons 'bound in marriage', and it is important for a host of reasons, to maintain the unity of the spouses. (Select Committee Report, 1975, 366)

The second example is taken from the Memorandum of Evidence from the Home Office, in a discussion of the fact that the then Criminal Injuries Compensation Scheme excluded injuries inflicted among members of the same family.

It can perhaps be argued that the Government (or the police) cannot have the same responsibility for the day to day behaviour of members of a household within their own walls. Some disagreement may be inevitable within a family. Even a degree of minor violence may be normal in some homes. It can perhaps be argued that the point at which the State should intervene in family violence should be higher than that which is expected in the case of violence between strangers. Or even that the State has no particular responsibility for compensating those who suffer violence in circumstances which are largely (in the case of adult members of a family) under their own control. (Select Committee Report, 1975, 418)

Both these statements suggest that the intervention of the state is less appropriate when the individuals concerned are linked by family ties as opposed to being strangers, and when the incident takes place in a private rather than a public place. To question this is not to advocate that there should be a policeman in every bedroom nor is it to argue for the abolition of privacy or of domestic life. However, for our topic it is important to consider more carefully the ways in which the public-private boundary is defined; more specifically, it is important to consider *whose privacy* is being respected or violated in particular circumstances. We shall argue that the notion of privacy is not an absolute value, that some people's privacy appears to be more inviolate than other people's privacy, and that by looking at how 'the private' is defined and maintained we can understand a great deal about the nature of power relations in a particular society.

The differentiation of public from private has a long tradition in Western European political thought, though the strength of the divide has varied at different historical periods, in different cultures and for different social classes within cultures (Elshtain, 1981). Thus a central distinction in ancient Greek culture was that between the *oikos* or private household, and the *polis*, the public and structured body politic. The private person, or *idiot*, was a being of lower purpose, goodness, rationality and worth than the public citizen, or *polites*, who belonged to and participated in the life of the city. Both Plato and Aristotle saw the private as somehow less noble than the public and both suggested that in the good society the private would be subordinated to the public. The association of women, children, servants and slaves with the private world of the household, in contrast to the public world inhabited by freemen, served both to intensify inequality between male and female and to reinforce the distinction between public and private. Women were portrayed by Aristotle as occupying the 'realm of necessity', a realm supportive of but essentially inferior to the public world of the *polis*.

The differentiation of public from private can be seen running through political thought from the ancient Greeks to the present day. In Britain it was particularly powerful in the nineteenth century. In 1869 John Stuart Mill likened the contemporary position of women to one in which 'women are wholly under the rule of men, having no share at all in public concerns, and each in private being under the legal obligation of obedience to the man with whom she has associated her destiny'. Mill made a link between the contemporary position of women and the abuse to which many Victorian wives were subjected by their husbands: 'The vilest malefactor has some wretched woman tied to him, against whom he can commit any atrocity except killing her, and, if tolerably cautious, can do that without much danger of the legal penalty' (Mill, 1912,

431). Davidoff has documented the separation of spheres which took place at the beginning of the nineteenth century and which was expressed in the mid-Victorian ideal of 'home':

> home, like the village, was ideally sheltered and separated from the public life of power – political, economic, educational, scientific – this separation was doubly enforced by the physical walls of the house, by the physical boundaries extending to hedges, fences and walls surrounding its garden setting. The intensity of privacy was, of course, related to the core sexual relationship in marriage. The home, even more than the village, represented an extreme of the privacy in which individualism could flourish. If we look more closely, however, we will see that the individualism refers *only* to the orientation of the master/husband; the privacy was used by him when he cared to invoke it. (Davidoff *et al.*, 1976, 140)

It seems that the right to domestic privacy is more easily invoked and defended by some members of society than by others; this differential right to privacy is important in explaining the 'invisibility' of wife abuse in most societies and at most periods of history (May, 1978). The Younger Committee, in its report on privacy, said:

> We have conceived of the right of privacy as having two main aspects. The first of these is freedom from intrusion upon oneself, one's home, family and relationships. The second is privacy of information, that is the right to determine for oneself how and to what extent informa-tion about oneself is communicated to others. (Report of the Committee on Privacy, 1972, 10)

It is clear that many violent husbands have definitions of privacy similar to these in their minds when they protest against the 'intrusion' of police officers who have come in response to an appeal for help from the assaulted wife. It seems that the police are often more willing to protect women living in refuges than they are to protect women who are the victims of violence in their own homes. There is evidence, too, that the police are less willing to intervene between a couple who are married and living in the same house; they are more willing to intervene either when a couple are married but are living apart, or when a couple are living together but are not married (Pahl, 1982a).

In analysing what we have termed the 'differential right to privacy' it is important to take into account the nature of power relations in any particular social situation. A few examples will serve to make the point that some people's privacy is more effectively protected than other people's privacy. The well-meaning Victorian visitor who sought out the needy to offer advice and charity would have been affronted had the same needy people subsequently called on her to investigate her domestic competence. The liable relative officer from the social security department will enter the house of a woman who is suspected of cohabiting while claiming supplementary benefit much more readily than the Inland Revenue will send an official to invade the privacy of a company director. Social researchers find it much easier to arrange interviews with the poor than with the rich, as a glance along the shelves of the social science section of any university library will testify. And in the context of wife abuse the privacy of the husband may be respected at the expense of the well-being of 'his' wife. This can be particularly important in very unequal marriages where the husband sees himself as head of the household and perceives his welfare as synony-mous with the welfare of the household as a whole. It is in just these sorts of marriages that the husband is likely to resent invasions of his privacy and agencies are likely to find it hardest to intervene. The husband can invoke the value of privacy in order to maintain his control over the domain defined as private. (For an extended discussion of the nature of power relations implicit in distinctions between the public and the private sphere, see Gamarnikow *et al.*, 1983).

In conclusion, then, there are two points to be made in considering the specific problem of wife abuse in the context of the more general issue of the public and the private. Firstly, the fact that wives are abused within the privacy of the home and within marriage alters the way in which the problem is perceived and the way in which agencies respond. The contributors to Part II of this book draw on their own research to expand and illuminate this point, with particular reference to the ways in which different agencies respond to requests for help from battered women. Whether the agency under consideration is the police (Faragher), the personal social services (Maynard, and Dobash, Dobash and Cavanagh), the housing department (Binney, Harkell and Nixon) or the health service (Dobash, Dobash and Caranagh) it is apparent that the help which is offered is patterned by assumptions about the nature of marriage and of family life. These assumptions often seem to prevent women from receiving the help to which they are legally entitled, and so the chapter by Parker is placed at the beginning of Part II in order to set out the legal framework within which help can be offered to the victims of wife abuse.

Secondly, it is important to remember that the public-private boundary is not rigidly defined. Its definition varies from one society to another, from one historical period to another and, within any one society at any one time, from one social group to another. The evidence from anthropology is particularly relevant here; much of this evidence was summarised by Rosaldo as follows:

> The model leads me to suggest, first, that women's status will be lowest in those societies where there is a firm differentiation between domestic and public spheres of activity and where women are isolated from one another and placed under a single man's authority, in the home. Their position is raised when they can challenge those claims to authority, either by taking on men's roles or by establishing social ties, by creating a sense of rank, order, and value in a world in which women prevail. One possibility for women, then, is to enter the men's world or to create a public world of their own. But perhaps the most egalitarian societies are those in which public and domestic spheres are only weakly differentiated, where neither sex claims much authority and the focus of social life itself is the home. (Rosaldo, in Rosaldo and Lamphere, 1974, 36)

It is the argument of this book that it is impossible to understand the nature of wife abuse without taking account of the social and ideological context within which it occurs. In attempting to help abused women it is important to recognise the taken-for-granted assumptions about marriage and the family which shape the ways in which women are defined. Ideas about marriage and the family are inextricably linked, at least in Western European thought, with ideas about privacy, and an emphasis on 'protecting privacy' can work to the detriment of those who are weakest within the social and physical space defined as private.

PART I

Violent husbands and abused wives: a longitudinal study

Jan Pahl

'I sometimes feel rather bitter, that I have been left the whole burden of bringing up the children – that's sometimes when I feel a little lonely. But it's nothing compared with the loneliness of being kicked out of bed, and going to sleep in another room, and being knocked over as he passes by, and cooking his meals and never getting so much as a good morning or a thank you and then being punched in the face as he passes by. That really is the epitome of loneliness.' (Interview with Jane)

Chapter two

Introduction to the study

Part I of this book presents the information which was collected from forty-two women whose husbands had been so violent to them that they had been forced to leave home. The study took place between 1976 and 1980, and was based in a refuge for abused women, known at the time as the Women's Centre. Each woman who took part in the study was interviewed twice. The first interview took place a few days after she had arrived at the refuge, while the second interview occurred about two years later, long after each women had left the refuge and had built a new life for herself and her children.

The initiative for the study came originally from the Homelessness and Addictions Research Liaison Group of the Department of Health and Social Security. In 1975 the Report from the Select Committee on Violence in Marriage had emphasised the lack of knowledge about this problem: 'The whole of the enquiry is being limited by the remarkable paucity of information about domestic violence' (Select Committee Report, 1975, xxiii). The Committee stressed the urgent need for research and hoped that 'the D.H.S.S. will hold more multi-disciplinary conferences, meetings and discussions, so that those with expertise can pool and publicise what knowledge is available' (xxiv). In the following years the Department funded a number of studies which investigated different aspects of the problem (see Dawson and Faragher, 1977; Delamont and Ellis, 1979; Dobash and Dobash, 1979; Dobash and Dobash, 1980; Elsey, 1980; Leonard and McLeod, 1980; Murch, 1981).

The majority of these studies focused on the ways in which different agencies perceived the problem and on the responses of social workers, doctors, health visitors, the police and others to requests for help from battered women; a minority of the studies focused on the women themselves, carrying out interviews in refuges in different parts of Britain, and documenting how the women perceived their problems and how they evaluated the help which they received, or did not receive. However, the study reported here is the only one which adopted a longitudinal approach, looking not only at what brought each woman to the refuge but at what happened to her when she left it, and investigating what she thought about the refuge not only when she had just arrived there, but afterwards, when each could set her stay at the refuge in the context of a crucial three or four years of her life. The study which is most comparable with that described here was carried out by the Women's Aid Federation/Department of the Environment Research Team between 1977 and 1980. This large-scale study involved interviewing 656 women in refuges all over England and Wales, and then re-interviewing a representative sub-sample of eighty-four women after they had left the refuges. The study was chiefly concerned with the housing needs of battered women, but a great deal of information was collected about many different aspects of the women's lives. In many ways the study done by the National Women's Aid Federation and that described in this report are complementary; where the areas of investigation overlap, the findings are remarkably similar (Binney, Harkell and Nixon, 1980a and 1981;Binney, 1981).

The study described in Part I of this book had three main aims. Firstly, it aimed to document what happened to the women and their children before, during and after their stay at the refuge. The focus here was on the particular pattern of structured constraints within which each woman had to make decisions about the future of herself and her children. Thus the interviews were designed to collect information not only about each woman's marital and family relationships, but also about her housing, her employment, and her financial situation, and about any difficulties which she was facing in any of these areas. Secondly, the study was concerned with each woman's attempts to get help with her difficulties and with her evaluation of any 'solutions' which she had been offered by her family and friends, by agencies such as the social services, the police, and the housing department, or by members of the medical and legal professions. The approach here was essentially subjective: 'helpfulness' was not defined by any objective criteria but by the women themselves. However, there is a validity in such 'actors' accounts': if people define situations as real they are real in their consequences. Thirdly, the study was concerned with the refuge itself. It was hypothesised that the refuge would serve different functions for different groups of women. Thus in the original research proposal it was suggested that 'one woman may go to the refuge for a short break from the strains of her marriage in order that it should continue, while another will go in order to get custody of the children and accommodation until her divorce is arranged. One woman may need only accommodation: another may need weeks of sympathy, support and practical help of many different sorts.' The interviews explored each woman's feelings about the refuge and about the help which she received there, and considered the extent to which women were involved in day-to-day decision making in the refuge. Women's Aid refuges, including the one in which this study was carried out, stress the importance of mutual support and self-help among the women and the desirability of women taking a share in the running of the organisation. It was hypothesised that such involvement fosters feelings of self-confidence and personal autonomy which help a woman to cope with her problems after leaving the refuge (Pahl, 1985).

This was a unique study in that it investigated marital breakdown, not retrospectively and after it had ended in divorce or separation, but as it was experienced by a group of women during the time when they were considering whether the breakdown should be temporary or permanent. When they were first interviewed all the women had ended, or were contemplating ending, their relationships with the men with whom they were living. (The word 'husband' will be used to refer to these men, even though some of the women were battered by men with whom they were cohabiting, and others by their ex-husbands; however, all the couples had at some time lived in a marriage-like relationship and so 'husband' seems the most appropriate noun to use.) After leaving the refuge sixteen of the women returned to their husbands, and in the time between the two interviews another six made at least one attempt each at reconciliation; altogether, in the time between the interviews these twenty-two women made a total of fifty-one attempts at reconciliation. However, by the time of the second interview, only nine of the women were still living with their husbands; nine had made new stable relationships and were living with a different man; and twenty-four were living on their own, usually with their children.

The study had two parts. The first took place in 1976, and involved interviewing nine of the women who planned and set up the Women's Centre and twenty-five of the women who stayed there (Pahl, 1978). During the whole of this part of the study the refuge was situated in a large and dilapidated house, occupied as a squat by the group which took the initiative in setting up the Women's Centre. The second part of the study ran from 1977 to 1980 and enlarged and extended the scope of the first part. By this time the refuge was housed in a smaller and more modern house which was rented to the group by the Local Authority Housing Department. The sample of women was enlarged by interviewing another twenty-five women at the new refuge, so that a total of fifty women had by then been drawn into the study. However, the first part of the study had made it clear that it was difficult to draw firm conclusions from the snapshot view of each woman's problems which was all that could be obtained from a single interview, carried out at a time when the woman was likely to be both distressed by what had happened to her and confused about what she should do in the future. Thus it was decided to extend the study over time by re-interviewing all the women after they had left the refuge. There was considerable anxiety about the feasibility of this: the women's homes were scattered over a wide geographical area; many were afraid of going back to the matrimonial home and hoped to be rehoused elsewhere; it was feared that some would be reluctant to be reminded of a distressing period in their lives by the arrival of an interviewer. However, I took pains to keep in touch with the women, by corresponding, by sending cards at Christmas and by visiting them when I could. In the end follow-up interviews were completed with forty-two women, 84 per cent of the original fifty, and outline information was collected about the majority of the missing eight. There were no refusals at the refuge. At the follow-up stage there were two refusals, and a further six women were not re-interviewed for a variety of different reasons. Of these six, two women were lost, two were living so far away that contacting them was impracticable and one became too ill to be interviewed; though the eighth woman wanted to be interviewed, the man who battered her was still living with her, he returned frequently to the house to check on her movements, and he would certainly not have permitted the interview, so she also dropped out of the follow-up study. There seemed to be few differences between the eight woman who were only interviewed once and the forty-two who are the subject of the main study. Though one might have expected that a woman who had returned to the man who battered her would be unwilling to be re-interviewed, in general this was not found to be so: the proportion of women who had returned to their husbands, and who were still with them at the time when the second interview was due to take place, was the same in the group with one interview as it was among the women who were interviewed twice. Structured and standardised question-naires were used for the interviews and these are available on request to the researcher. However, the interviews were usually extremely informal, more conversational than inter-rogative. All the interviews were tape recorded; each question-naire was filled in after the interview had ended, and selected parts of each recording were transcribed verbatim; the quotations used in this report are taken from these transcriptions.

Inevitably the study raised many broader issues. Of central concern to this book is the question of privacy. Violence within marriage is seen as essentially a private matter, both by the man and woman concerned and by those outside the marriage. If this privacy is maintained and respected, what are the implications of this for the people concerned, which include not just the husband and wife, but also their children? Who is being protected when privacy is respected? At what point, and at whose request, is it appropriate for public agencies to intervene in the private world of marriage? The study raised broader issues, too, about both the nature of marriage and the role of the welfare state. For example, to what extent is a woman with young children trapped in a violent marriage, not by anything within herself, but by social and economic constraints in the wider society which affect all married women with children to a greater or lesser extent? How can the bureaucracies of the welfare state, set up to deal with specific problems in specific parts of people's lives, provide help when the real problems of any one individual do not come neatly packaged for the bureaucratic categories but in a confused tangle of overlapping needs and responsibilities? Such questions raise issues of fundamental importance to which we shall return in Part II.

Chapter three

Marital violence and marital problems

This chapter will attempt to set the violence which each woman had experienced in the context of the relationship between her and her husband. What was the nature and the extent of the violence? What appeared to trigger off the assaults? To what extent was the violence associated with other marital problems? And what attempts had the women made in the past to escape from their marriages? This chapter will discuss these and other questions, with the aim of developing an understanding of the problems which the women were facing when they approached the refuge, and the statutory agencies, for help.

The violence which the women had experienced ranged from cuts and bruises, through black eyes, broken arms, noses and ribs, to a ruptured spleen and a fractured skull. Two examples will have to suffice to remind us of what an assault can be like when it actually happens. Doris's husband had his own small electrical business and she did all the bookkeeping for the firm; they have three young children. She said:

'He hits me whether he's sober or whether he's drunk.
But I believe that he will go out drinking first as a
punishment for me. It's hard to put it into words – it
seems silly to say it's punishment to me and yet it always
works that way. I know that if he comes home and there
is an argument, he always says, "I'm off to the pub – I've
had enough of this". And I know that if I can keep my
own temper I will beg him not to go, because I know that
if he does go then I always do get in a lot more trouble.

'Anyway, I was very tired that night and I went to bed early. Then he came to bed, and my little girl woke up, because she'd wet the bed. Anyway I went to see to her and I took the sheet and I moved it round so that I moved her off the wet part. And I went back to bed. Anyway she cried again and he went out to see to her. And I didn't know what had hit me. He came in and he ripped the clothes off me and grabbed me by the feet, and dragged me out of bed. And he kicked me out into the hall and he called me all these names, and he said, "How dare you leave that child with a wet sheet on the bed." And he threw me into her bedroom. So I did the little girl, changed the bed all right round again, and then I went into the bathroom and locked the door, because I was so upset. He came in and knocked the bolt off and he dragged me back into our bedroom to make the bed. And I remember I had my dressing gown on and he threw me all the way down the hall and he ripped my dressing gown and then he threw me on the floor and he was kicking me and I was sitting there screaming. And then he said he'd give me half an hour and then I was to go back into the bedroom and I was to apologise and he meant apologise properly. He put one arm round my throat, and he slapped me and punched me and he said, "How dare you look at me as if I'm repulsive to you. You're my wife, and I'll do what the bloody hell I like to you." '

Suzy's husband is a painter and decorator, but he has been out of work for some time. They have four very young children. She said:

'He never looks after the kids; he'll take Lisa for a little sometimes but he won't help me round the house or nothing like that. He hasn't got a job – he hasn't worked for two or three years. So he's sitting round the house, flicking his ash on the floor, which gets on my nerves, making me make cups of coffee all day long. I don't mind doing it, but he's so lazy; he never says, "You put your feet up, and I'll make a cup of coffee." So I'm working from the time I get up, which is early, till the time I go to bed. And then sometimes, if he's still awake, he says,

"Come down and make up a cup of coffee." That's part of
the trouble, because he says that I'm lazy because I want
to sleep at three o'clock in the morning.

'He beat me up once in front of my sister. I was
pregnant, six months pregnant, and it was Lisa's birthday
party. And he asked me to make him a cup of tea, and I
was doing the party things. So I said, "Well, wait a
minute." And he said, "I told you to do it now." And I
said, "Well, wait five minutes." I had long hair, and he
took hold of the end of the plait, and twisted it round
like that, and just threw me against the cupboard. And he
took hold of my head and just banged it against the wall;
he just banged and banged. They took me into hospital in
an ambulance, and when I heard the siren going I said,
"I've only got a cut, you know." "Only got a cut!" they
said, "Have you seen your face? You're just one mass of
bruises. Your eye's black, and you've got a great big gash
up there on your head." And they stitched it all up and
everything, and then they took an X-ray.'

These two brief statements contain within them references
to many different elements which might be seen as 'causing',
or as being associated in some way with the violence:
excessive consumption of alcohol, disputes over meals and
meal times, jealousy, differing expectations about the way the
spouse should perform the role of husband or of wife,
unemployment, possessiveness, and so on. What links are
there between such elements and a husband's ill-treatment of
his wife? This particular study was not concerned so much
with the causes of marital violence as with the responses of
wives who found themselves living with a violent husband.
However, it may be useful to compare the explanations and
accounts which were given by the women with the more
general explanations of violence against wives which were
discussed in Chapter 1.

How, then, did the women in this case study explain the
violence which had happened to them? They were asked both
about the cause of the incident which led them to leave home
and come to the refuge, and also about the other problems in
their married lives which might have precipitated or exacerbated the violence, or which were simply among the

Table 3.1: Cause of the incident which forced the woman to leave

N = 42	% giving as cause or part of cause
Alcohol	31
Personality problems	31
Jealousy	26
Expectations over performance of roles	24
One partner going out without the other	24
Sex	17
Money	14
Meals and mealtimes	10

difficulties with which they had to contend. In many ways the two sets of answers complement each other. The reasons given by the women for their husbands' most recent act of violence against them are shown in Table 3.1; they were, in order of the frequency with which they were mentioned, his drinking too much, his abnormally aggressive personality, his jealousy, and his unrealistic expectations of the ways in which she would perform the role of wife. Many disputes seemed to centre around a double standard in which the husband expected to be able to go out alone, but would not allow his wife to do the same. Thus Emma said of her police officer husband:

'He's very jealous. If we go out for lunch or go out for a drink, or something, all the time he's watching me – if I go to talk to someone, he's watching. But if he gets up he can talk to who he likes. It isn't as if I go chatting all the men up or anything, but if a friend comes up and speaks to you, you can't exactly turn round and say, "I'm awfully sorry, I can't talk to you, my husband doesn't like it." And I just cannot make it out, why he should be allowed to go out and I shouldn't. He says to me, "Oh, well, its different if I go out, I don't know what you'll be doing. And I'm not going to have people coming and saying, I saw Emma, talking to such and such a person."
'I think he's just got a bit of a chip on his shoulder and

he can't express love; he's not a really affectionate
person, if you know what I mean. It's very hard for him
to show it and I think somewhere along the line we've
both got confused. He doesn't quite know how to
approach me, and so he shouts at me instead.'

When they described their marriages in broader terms it was
clear that in many cases the violence was only one element in
marriages which were troubled in many other ways, as Table
3.2 shows. Money had been a problem area for 79 per cent of
the women, 52 per cent said that their husband had drunk
excessively, 45 per cent said that their husband's jealous and
dominating behaviour had been a problem; 45 per cent said
that their difficulties had been exacerbated by inadequate
housing; and 43 per cent of the husbands had at one time or
another been in trouble with the law. Let us consider some of
these areas separately.

Table 3.2: Marital problems before going to the refuge

N = 42	% of women reporting as a problem*
Violence by husband towards wife	98
Violence by husband towards children	36
Disputes over money	79
Husband drinking excessively	52
Husband's jealousy/dominance	45
Housing difficulties	45
Husband in trouble with the law	33
Husband unemployed	24

*Percentages add up to more than 100 because of women giving more than
one answer.

Money and dependence

There is now a considerable body of evidence to suggest that
marital breakdown is associated wth inequitable patterns of

allocation of money within the household. Studies of divorced and separated women consistently report a substantial proportion of such women as saying that they are 'better off' living on supplementary benefit than they had been when they were living with their husbands. The proportion saying this varies from 18 per cent (Houghton, 1973), through 33 per cent (Marsden, 1973), to 65 per cent (Binney, Harkell and Nixon, 1980a). Since supplementary benefit levels are normally taken to represent the poverty level in Britain, this finding implies that these women, and probably their children, were living below the poverty line before the marriage broke down. It must be emphasised that this does not necessarily mean that the total household income was inadequate: in many cases the money coming into the house would have been enough to keep all the members of the family comfortably. Hidden, intra-household poverty of this sort is the result of the inequitable allocation of the household income. It is not yet clear whether such inequitable allocation is the cause, or the effect, of the marriage breaking down; however, the fact that it occurs so frequently has important implications for all those who are concerned with income maintenance and who may be approached for help by women considering divorce or separation. The difficulties such women face are compounded by the fact that, like many married women, they have long used up any savings which they had at the time of their wedding, and have been unable to acquire any in the course of their married lives, so that when they are forced to leave home they become completely and immediately dependent on the support of the state.

The question of the allocation of money within the household is an extremely complicated one, which is particularly important when the children are young and they and their mother are likely to be financially dependent on the father/breadwinner (Pahl, 1980 and 1983). It is important to consider not only how much of his income the husband transfers to his wife, but also what she has to pay out of the money. At the beginning of the study the control and allocation of money were not seen as being important: it was the women themselves who drew attention to this topic in the course of the first set of interviews. For example, when asked how she liked living at the refuge Annette replied:

'One thing, I've found, since we've been here, my little girl's started to sleep all night. I think some of it is that we were that short of money that I couldn't give her as much to eat as what I can here. I've found that actually now I'm on my own with Mandy – I'm financially better off. I'm one of those – I have to work everything out before I spend any money. I never go shopping without a shopping list, and I only buy what is on the list. When I got my money, I used to put my rent away, put my milk money away, put my money away for the electricity, put my money away for the gas bottles. That's what used to annoy me – he used to spend £4 a week on cigarettes, and I said, "They don't allow you for that. That's coming out of money they allow us for food and that." I said, "You're more or less smoking half our food money." '

Accordingly, in the second set of interviews at the refuge the women were asked systematically about how they and their husbands had divided their money, about the housekeeping allowances the women had received from their husbands, and about the items of household expenditure for which the women had been responsible. Out of the twenty-five women who were asked this series of questions, five were basically responsible for managing the household finances, though all of these women gave their husbands some money for their personal use; four of these households were living on social security. It is interesting that other studies have also suggested that in households which are dependent on supplementary benefit the woman is more likely to be responsible for budgeting: when money is short having one person responsible for the household's finances helps to make sure that all the bills get paid (Land, 1969; Pahl, 1980). Two couples operated a pooling system for their money, putting their earnings together and sharing the control and allocation of the money.

In five of the twenty-five households the wife received no money at all. In one instance this was because the husband was the owner of a café; his wife, who worked in the café, was expected to eat all her meals there and she and their three children were clothed by her parents. For those wives who were not given any money the most usual pattern was for the

35

couple to go shopping together on a 'family shopping night'; the wife would choose the goods which the household needed and the husband would pay for them at the checkout. Thus what at first sight looks like the symmetrical family at its most egalitarian, with husband and wife doing the shopping together, may in some cases represent a particularly inegalitarian form of marital relationship, with the wife kept in a state of perpetual financial dependence.

In the remaining thirteen households the husband retained control of the income but delegated responsibility for the expenditure of parts of it to his wife. Here the pattern is very complicated since not only do the amounts which wives are given vary, but their financial responsibilities vary too, and the amount which a woman receives may be plenty to pay the bills which are her responsibility or may be extremely inadequate.

Control of the money often appeared as one element in a marital relationship in which the husband assumed that he would be the dominant partner. This finding lends support to the analysis of wife battering which sees the violence as a concomitant of the structured inequality between men and women both in marriage and in the wider society. Many women described how their husbands seemed to use control of the money as part of a more general attempt to control and subordinate them. In her first interview, at the refuge, Emma described how her husband used to give her 'a pound or two occasionally for tights', out of his wages of over £100 per week; he paid all the bills and did all the shopping, except when he was away. In her second interview she desribed an incident which occurred at the end of a brief attempt at reconciliation after she left the refuge:

> 'I said, "Can't you leave us some money, for food?" "No, I
> can't," he said. So he just ran across the road to the van
> with his friend; so I ran out after him, and this friend
> said, "Come on, Peter, give Emma some money for some
> food." And then he said, "All right, I will." And he
> opened his wallet – he had a great big wad of notes – he
> just picked out one pound note, just slung it on the
> ground, didn't give it to me, just slung it on the ground.
> It was humiliating standing out there, I'd just had

enough. So I said, "Right, Peter, that's enough; when you come home, I'm not going to be here." And of course he laughed, all ha ha ha, where do you think you're going to go, and all this. And it just clicked me . . . so I packed some things there and then and left. And we camped in a field.'

Some husbands used their wife's financial dependence to prolong the marriage, and this was particularly effective when the wife had few alternative sources of help. Lisa had come from a Mediterranean country, had left all her family behind, and had not been allowed to make new friends. Her story illustrates the crucial role which women's refuges have played in enabling women to leave their violent husbands:

'I wanted to leave my husband a long time ago – but I'd got nowhere to go. Five or six years ago there wasn't a Women's aid about, was there? I haven't got anyone in this country that I could turn to: I've got friends – which are all his friends. I warned my husband many many times that I was going to leave him, but he knew that I'd got nowhere to go. He won't give me no money to save up, so I can't go back to my own country. If I could go back to my country, I wouldn't come back. But he wouldn't give me any money. He said that any time I wanted to leave I'd never make the door – he'd do me in before I reached the door.'

The links between wife battering and disputes over money and over the wife's right to personal autonomy have also been found by other researchers. The Dobashes, in their study of 109 battered women, found that 'the majority of the disputes that preceded the violence focused on the husband's jealousy of his wife, differing expectations regarding the wife's domestic duties, and the allocation of money' (Dobash and Dobash, 1980, 98). Roy, in her study of 150 American women who had sought help because of their husbands' violence, found that the four factors which most often led to violent confrontation were, in order of importance, arguments over money, jealousy, sexual problems and alcohol (Roy, 1977, 40).

In her study *Hidden Violence*, Evason made important links between wife abuse on the one hand and the nature of marriage on the other hand, with particular emphasis on financial arrangements within marriage (Evason, 1982). Evason interviewed 694 single parents living in Northern Ireland; of these 277 (40 per cent) were divorced or separated women, of which 155 (56 per cent) had been battered wives. The discovery that more than half of these divorced or separated women had been victims of wife abuse is itself important, especially with the growth in the rates of marital breakdown. Evason's study showed that violence against wives cannot be discussed as an isolated, atypical problem, but that it should instead be seen as a fairly common feature of husband-wife relationships, especially among those that end in divorce or separation.

Evason's study focused on the differences between the group of women who had been battered by their husbands and those who had not. There were no differences between the two groups in terms of education and social class, or in terms of how long the partners had known each other before marrying, or their ages at marriage. Significant differences appeared between the two groups, however, when attention was focused on the nature of these marriages and on the spouses' expectations and assumptions. The great majority of all the wives would have liked a democratic model of marriage with decisions made jointly; by contrast, husbands were seen by their wives as much more likely to favour the traditional, male-dominant model of marriage, in which a husband is 'master in his home'. Violent husbands were particularly likely to favour the traditional model, 66 per cent of them favouring male dominance, compared with 34 per cent of the non-violent husbands.

There were further differences between the two groups of women in the ways in which the couples had organised their money. Evason distinguishes three models of money management; these were, firstly, joint management, secondly, the model in which a housekeeping allowance is paid to the wife by the husband, and a third model in which the husband controls the finances and allocates money to his wife if and when he sees fit to do so. Just under half of all the couples adopted the housekeeping allowances model. However, violent husbands were more likely to adopt the third model and less likely to use joint management than were non-violent

husbands. Evason ends by identifying the financial dependence of married women as an important part of the pattern of
structured constraints which keeps women within violent
marriages. (See also Homer, Leonard and Taylor, 1984.)

The fact that financial arrangements are seen as a very
private part of a couple's life together is not irrelevant. It
seems likely that one function of this norm of privacy is to
maintain particular power relations within the family, power
relations which are reflected and reinforced in patterns of
allocation of money. The maintenance of privacy in this very
central sphere serves to protect the domestic status quo
against invasion by alternative norms from outside the
household.

Alcohol and violence

Many studies have suggested a close association between
battering and the consumption of alcohol: 52 per cent of the
women said that their husbands drank excessively and it was
clear that many felt there was a link between their husband's
consumption of alcohol and his violent behaviour. Gelles, in
his study of violence in New Hampshire, found that drinking
accompanied violence in 48 per cent of the families where
assaults had occurred. Many of the wives in his sample said
that their husbands only hit them when drunk. The association seemed to be a peculiarly male one, since only one wife
in the sample became violent to her husband or children
when inebriated (Gelles, 1974). In his study of 100 women
who stayed at the Chiswick refuge, Gayford found that 52 per
cent of the women said that their husband was drunk at least
once a week, and another 22 per cent said that he was drunk at
least once a month; 44 per cent reported that the violence only
occurred when the man was under the influence of alcohol
(Gayford, 1975). Additionally, there is evidence from work on
alcoholism that male alcoholics are likely to ill-treat their
wives. Scott reports the results of a study in which the wives
of 100 male alcoholics were interviewed. The marital problems which they reported are very similar to the problems
reported by battered women. Seventy-two per cent of the
women said that their husbands sometimes threatened them,

45 per cent said that they had been beaten by their husbands, 27 per cent said that their husbands had attempted to kill or seriously injure them, and 49 per cent said that their husbands were possessive and jealous, asking questions about everyone they met (Scott, 1974).

However, it has been suggested that drunkenness should not be seen as a 'cause' of violence, but rather as a condition which sometimes co-exists with it. The Dobashes found that the husband's drinking behaviour was insignificant as a source of conflict, though 25 per cent of the women said that their husband was often drunk when assaults took place (Dobash and Dobash, 1980). It appears that the link between violent behaviour and excessive consumption of alcohol is extremely complicated, and that it is likely that *both* are related to more fundamental conflicts within the marriage. Gelles suggests that 'individuals who wish to carry out a violent act become intoxicated in order to carry out the violent act' (Gelles, 1974, 117). Gayford's study gave some support to this analysis: the women whom he interviewed often reported that a trivial row would precede a husband's heavy drinking bout. He would leave home in an angry mood and violence would occur on his return home; the next day both he and his wife could excuse his behaviour on the grounds that he had been drunk and could therefore not be held responsible for his behaviour; some husbands even claimed that they could not remember anything about the event (Gayford, 1975). My own conclusion is that excessive consumption of alcohol is best understood not so much as a 'cause' of violence but as an excuse for it: as Doris, who was quoted at the beginning of this chapter, said, 'He hits me whether he's sober or whether he's drunk. But I believe that he will go out drinking first as a punishment for me.'

Other problems

The problem of housing, as it affects abused women in general, is dealt with in detail in chapter 11. Here the aim is simply to consider the extent to which housing was a problem for the forty-two women who were interviewed in the course of this study.

Housing difficulties were a problem for the women in two different ways. Firstly, 45 per cent of the women said that inadequate or unsuitable housing had exacerbated the difficulties which the couple were already experiencing in their married lives. Many of the couples had spent months living with parents; others had lived in privately rented accommodation while waiting for a council house: in many cases they could not afford more than one or two rooms; in two cases, they had been living in a caravan. Six of the forty-two were actually homeless, or were living in local authority homeless family accommodation, immediately before the woman came to the refuge. The homeless family accommodation usually consisted of a single room, or bed and breakfast accommodation, and this imposed great strains on young couples, cooped up with babies and small children and with inadequate financial resources. When a couple have spent many nights sharing a room with a fretful baby and a restless, anxious toddler, it is hardly surprising that trivial disagreements escalate quickly to major rows.

Secondly, housing was a problem for women who wanted to leave their violent husbands, either to reconsider and renegotiate their marriages, or to start a new life elsewhere. Eighty-six per cent had made attempts to leave their husbands before coming to the refuge, half of these having left more than four times. The women were asked about the longest of these pre-refuge separations, about where they went and why they eventually returned. Here the crucial importance of housing need in forcing women to return to violent husbands becomes clear. When the women left home they most commonly took the children and went to stay with their parents or other close relatives (39 per cent), or with friends (22 per cent); some had spent time in other refuges, and a few had found privately rented accommodation. Only a third of these attempts to leave lasted for more than a month; in many cases the women only stayed away for a few days. Their reasons for going back were primarily to do with accommodation. Some women could not find anywhere for themselves and their children to live; some felt that they could not continue to impose themselves on other households; some simply missed their own homes. Altogether, 36 per cent of those who returned home did so because of reasons connected with accommodation; 31 per cent returned home for the sake of the children; and 22 per cent returned because they had been persuaded to do so by husbands who pleaded for forgiveness, who promised to reform, or who threatened them with further violence if they stayed away. The majority of the first interviews were carried out before the Housing (Homeless Persons) Act came into force in 1977; however, the interviews provide ample evidence of the need for this Act and of its importance in securing safe, adequate accommodation for battered women and their children.

Finally, it seemed that there might be an association between the violence and the unemployment of the husband. Twenty-four per cent of the men were out of work when they committed the assault which forced their wives to go to the refuge; this was at a time when the unemployment rate in Britain was around 6 per cent. A number of studies have documented the damaging effects which unemployment can have on individuals and the impact on the families in which they live. Studies carried out in the 1930s showed that unemployment can be the cause of considerable stress because of its impact on family living standards and on the mental and physical health of the unemployed person (Jahoda *et al.*, 1972; Bakke, 1933; Angel, 1936). An interesting finding of the work by Komarovsky was that American families responded in one of two ways to unemployment. In some, the effect of the chief earner losing his job was an increase in family solidarity and an increased flexibility in work roles within the household; in other families, however, unemployment was associated with stress and marital breakdown (Komarovsky, 1940).

More recently research on this topic has been concerned with the unemployment of the late 1970s and the early 1980s. The work of Brenner lends support to the idea that there are links between unemployment and psychological impairment, and a number of other studies suggest that, not only is there a risk to the unemployed person, but that this risk extends to the family and to the wider community during a recession (Brenner, 1977; Colledge, 1982). There are reports of increased strain and tension within families where the chief earner is out of work: 'Budget reductions and over-proximity caused frequent tensions between family members, occasionally leading to violence, divorce and family break-ups' (Colledge and Bartholomew, 1980; see also Hill, 1978; Showler and Sinfield, 1981; Popay, 1981; Fagin and Little, 1984).

The study described in Part I of this book was not concerned with the causes of violence so much as with its effects. However, the evidence suggests that the violent behaviour of many husbands grew out of a combination of two elements, of which unemployment was often one. The first element is the assumption on the husband's side that marriage is, and should be, an unequal relationship in which he, the husband, should be dominant; the second element is the realisation that in some way or other he is in reality unable to play the dominant role to which he aspires, because, for example, he is unemployed. If this dual-causation hypothesis is correct, it implies that long-term solutions to the problem of violence against wives will require profound changes, particularly in the patterns of relationships within the family.

Chapter four

Marriage and marriage breakdown

All research begins with certain assumptions, many of which will be proved to be wholly or partly wrong as the study proceeds. This chapter is concerned with two such assumptions. The first was that the stay at the refuge would mark a turning point in the women's lives and that after it each woman would either return to her husband or would leave him and make a new life for herself on her own. A second and related assumption was that after they left the refuge it would be possible to divide the women into two groups, one containing those who had returned to their husbands and one containing those whose marriages had ended. Both these assumptions proved to be true, but also to be over-simplifications of what actually happened

This chapter will present background information about the women, and about their husbands and children; it will then go on to describe what happened to these forty-two families during the three or four years of the study and to discuss the accounts which the women gave of the decisions which they made on behalf of themselves and their children. The aim of the chapter is to set the scene for the discussion, in the following chapters, of the women's experiences at the refuge and after leaving it and of their attempts to get help from their families and friends and from the statutory and voluntary agencies.

Patterns of marriage

There are a number of general points which need to be made about the women, and about the relationships which they had left. Firstly, the women were leaving relationships which had endured for many years, after putting up with prolonged violence; as Tables 4.1, 4.2 and 4.3 show these were not very young women, precipitately leaving their marriages at the first appearance of trouble. At the time of the first interview the majority of the women were in their twenties or early thirties; 52 per cent were aged between 20 and 29, and another 29 per cent were between 30 and 34. In general they were leaving quite long-standing relationships: 50 per cent of the women had been with their violent partner for at least six years, and only 12 per cent of the couples had been together for less than two years. In the majority of cases the violence too was long-standing. Sixty-two per cent of the women said that the violence had gone on for three or more years, a proportion which is confirmed by the National Women's Aid Federation which found 73 per cent of the women reporting violence which had persisted for at least three years (Binney, Harkell and Nixon, 1980a).

Secondly, the couples were drawn from all social classes, with the exception only of the professional and managerial classes. However, there are many problems about this finding. There are difficulties about saying anything about the social class of married women, especially when they have dependent children, as did most of the women. The expectation that they will be responsible for child care and domestic work either prevents them from taking any paid employment, or forces them into a double burden of paid and unpaid work which militates against their taking on any but part-time and badly paid employment. The social processes which trap married women in the secondary labour market have been discussed elsewhere (Amsden, 1980; Barron and Norris, 1976; Bruegel, 1979). In the year before they came to the refuge, 48 per cent of the women had paid employment, a higher proportion than would be expected for married women in this age group: it seems likely that this increased rate of employment is related to the difficulties which the women had been facing, and particularly their financial difficulties.

Table 4.1: Duration of violence

N = 42	%
less than a year	12
one year but less than three years	26
three years but less than six years	33
six years and over	26
(did not apply)	2

Table 4.2: Ages of women at first interview

N = 42	%
24 or less	33
25 to 29	21
30 to 39	29
40 or more	17

Table 4.3: Duration of relationship with husband

N = 42	%
Under 2 years	12
2 years to under 4 years	19
4 years to under 6 years	17
6 years to under 8 years	14
8 years and over	36
(did not apply)	2

However, because the employment options open to them were so constrained by their domestic circumstances, most of the women were doing unskilled and casual work. Some studies have dealt with this problem by classifying married women according to their husbands' occupations; however, this did

Table 4.4: Socio-economic status of women in the study and their husbands by comparison with total population of earners in Great Britain in 1977 (in percentages)

| | Men | | Women | |
	in study	in Britain*	in study	in Britain*
Professional, employers and managers	0	21	0	5
Intermediate and junior non-manual	17	18	43	51
Skilled manual and own account non-professional	43	41	12	8
Semi- and unskilled manual, personal service workers	40	20	45	36

*Source: Central Statistical Office, 1979.

not seem appropriate in this case. I have therefore chosen to classify the women according to their own occupations, or according to their last occupation if they were unemployed. The results are set out in Table 4.4 and show, as well as the spread across the social scale, a tendency for there to be higher proportions of working-class, and particularly unskilled working-class people in the study families, when compared with the total population of Britain.

This leads on to another problem: that of interpreting these findings. Researchers in the field agree that wife battering occurs at every level of society, though little is known about its precise prevalence in the general population (Select Committee Report, 1975, xxiii; Marsden, 1978). However, it does seem as if wife battering is somewhat more common among lower socio-economic groups. Working-class women are certainly over-represented among women who go to refuges. This probably reflects a number of different factors, not only the higher divorce rate among working-class couples, but also the wider range of alternative sources of help available to middle-class women, who are more likely to have savings of their own, whose parents are more likely to be able to help them financially, and whose relatives more often have houses large enough to accommodate an extra family for some time. By comparison with working-class women, those middle-class women who did use the refuge were likely to have made longer and more determined efforts to leave their husbands in the past, and were less likely to return to their husbands after leaving the refuge.

Thirdly, it seemed as though there were links between the violence and the fact that the couple were married. Though it sometimes appeared as if the violence was related to the fact that the woman was pregnant, or was looking after a young baby, many women felt that it was marriage, rather than pregnancy, which had triggered violent reactions in their husbands. A number of women commented that, though they had lived happily together before being married, it was after they were married that the violence began. Doreen lost her baby when her husband kicked her downstairs when she was pregnant; however, the violence had begun when the couple were first married:

'We lived together for two years, which was lovely. And as soon as we got married I became a possession, not a person. I wasn't a person any longer. After he's knocked me about and I've moved into the spare room, he's always very very sorry . . . and in come bottles of perfume and all this. But as I said to him many times – you can't buy affection. And when they start knocking you about and you start losing teeth, and they start scarring you, and you break your nose and all that – just slowly the love dies out and you don't want to know.

'He's very insecure, I think, emotionally. I think one of the reasons he is so insecure is that he was divorced before and his first wife divorced him for exactly the same reasons – physical and mental cruelty. He doesn't seem to know why he does it. I think it's to try and exert his male . . . whatever they like to call it . . . superiority. He's always telling me that he's better than I am and all this load of old waffle. But then he's the first to admit that anything he can do I can do just as well. I mean, I've knocked up cement and laid it; I've put central heating in with him; I've re-wired a house; and I used to make all

the kids' clothes, my clothes, his clothes even I've made.
I'm fairly practical.'

Table 4.5: Ages of children at second interview

N = 124 *Age ranges*	*% of children in each age range*
0-4	26
5-10	49
11-15	19
16 and over	5

Responsibility for children

All the couples had children, since this was one criterion for
the inclusion of women in the study. More significantly, the
great majority of these children were very young, as Table 4.5
shows. As we have seen, most of the women put up with the
violence for many years before taking the drastic step of going
to a refuge. Often it was when the eldest child started to notice
what was going on that women decided that it was time to
leave home. Out of the forty-two couples there were thirty-
eight (90 per cent) who had a child under 5 in the family at
some time or other during the years when the violence was
taking place. If we look back to the time when the violence
first began there was a child under 2 in fourteen (33 per cent)
of the households; in another fourteen (33 per cent) of the
households the women was pregnant when the violence
began, and in one household she was both pregnant and had a
child under 2. Thus when the violence first began there was
either a child under 2, or the assaulted woman was pregnant,
in twenty-nine (69 per cent) of the households. Clearly health
visitors who routinely visit homes in which there are young
children are potentially one of the most immediately available
sources of help for battered women.

49

The children were one important reason why women endured the violence for so many years. Often the relationship between father and children was satisfactory: men who batter their wives do not normally batter their children; on the other hand men who batter their children are quite often also wife batterers. Women were unwilling to leave their children behind, yet they hesitated for a long time before removing them to the poverty and loneliness of life as a single-parent family, even though this would mean greater safety for themselves. As the years passed, however, it often became clear that the violence was affecting the children, either directly or indirectly. The welfare of the children was often an important reason for a woman deciding to leave her husband. Some women commented that, while they could endure the violence for themselves, it was when the children started to notice and to be upset by their father's behaviour that they decided that it was time to make a determined attempt to leave him. More seriously, 36 per cent of the women said that their husbands had battered one or more of their children, while 54 per cent of the women said that the children had been noticeably distressed by the marital problems of their parents.

The most common pattern was for the women to bring all their children to the refuge with them, and 76 per cent did this. The remainder left one or more of their children behind, usually with the children's father or with grandparents. The great majority of the children at the refuge were under 10 years old; however, the children who were left behind were likely to be older than this. In addition, a high proportion of the teenagers who came to the refuge left it again and went to live with friends or returned to their father. The question of children living in refuges is considered in chapter 12. By comparison with the general population of Britain, these families were rather larger than average, with a smaller proportion of one-child families and a larger proportion of families of four and more children. However, this difference was not great and the majority of the women (60 per cent) had either two or three children. The somewhat larger family size of the families using the refuge is best explained as a reflection of the difficulty in finding alternative accommodation: few households can take in four or five extra people for very long, and so for such families the refuge provided the only possible alternative to remaining with the violent man. In theory the passing of the Housing (Homeless Persons) Act should have solved this problem; however, it seems that some local authorities are still attempting to evade their responsibilities under the Act and so the problem of finding accommodation for families, and in particular for large families, remains acute in some areas.

The stay at the refuge

The refuge, and the women's experiences during their stay, have been described elsewhere (Pahl, 1985). Here it is only possible to describe briefly the use the women made of the refuge, in order to set their time there in the context of all the decisions which they made about their lives over the years when the study was taking place. The importance of the refuge varied enormously: one woman stayed a week and could remember little about it; another came as a bruised and unhappy woman, and stayed on to become one of the workers, playing a key role not only in making decisions within the support group, but also in representing the Women's Aid group to other agencies and organisations.

The length of time which the women spent at the refuge varied widely. Twenty-nine per cent stayed less than a month, and these women either returned to their husbands or were enabled to return to the matrimonial home by swift and effective legal action. A third of the women stayed for between one and three months. Finally, 35 per cent stayed for over three months; the great majority of these were women who were determined to leave their husbands, but who could not return to the matrimonial home and had to find other accommodation in which to live; a few of these stayed at the refuge for nearly a year.

The number of visits which the women paid to the refuge also varied, reflecting in part the different functions which it fulfilled. A minority of women (17 per cent) paid three or more visits, and for some of these the refuge, and the people who were most closely associated with it, became a crucial source of support and a key point in their social network. As

Vicky, rehoused just half a mile from the refuge, said:

'I've got no family as such; I've just got me and her (the
baby). She hasn't got a grandmother, she hasn't got
uncles and aunties and you know, cousins and things
which I had. Since I got married, they don't want to
know. My father died when I was 14, and my mother
went to Australia. I'm on my own. I feel sorry for her that
way; I don't feel sorry for myself any more. I used to but I
don't any more, because I've got so many friends; I've got
the refuge, and that's enough for me. I always know I've
got that place to go to, that's always there when I need it.'

A gipsy woman, who stayed at the refuge five times during
the course of the study, said, in her first interview at the
refuge:

'They spoke to me just like sisters, and they stuck by me.
It really broke my heart that I had somebody there to turn
to. I wouldn't care if I had thousands of friends – this
would be the first place I would turn to. As soon as you
come in you get a cup of tea. When they make a pot, it's
all shared round. If you've got no food or anything, they
say, "You can have a couple of slices of mine." I've never
met a beautifuller lot of people in my life. It's just like a
travellers' way – good travellers, I mean – they sort of
turn round and say, "Got no clothes? You can lend this
till you get some clothes for your children." If you're ill
or anything, they say, "Oh give me your child and I'll
wash and do for it." '

In her second interview, looking back on the refuge, she said:

'It was just like one big family, and I enjoyed it, because
you had all your meals together and they was all circled
round. Everybody helped one another, they all pulled the
same way, you all had a good laugh. It was fantastic. I
used to like new people coming in – I used to make them
a cup of tea, make them a bed up. It's a funny sensation
to explain to anybody . . . when you've been beat up, and
you've got to leave your own place, and you're going into
a different place – going in a refuge, you feel more
supported. You feel like you're in a circle, you've got
somebody to lean on.'

More commonly, however, the women only paid either one (52 per cent) or two (31 per cent) visits to the refuge. However, these visits might be very different in the importance which they had for the women. The original proposal for this study hypothesised that the refuge would fill a wide range of different functions for different women; the follow-up interviews showed that this original hypothesis was correct; when we look at what happened to the women after they left the refuge the full diversity of their lives becomes clear.

Leaving the refuge

The great advantage of a longitudinal study such as this is that it provides a much greater wealth of detail than does the one-off, snapshot type of study, and that it enables one to develop a much more profound understanding about the lives of the people who are the subjects of the study. The drawback is that the mass of detail may make it more difficult to discern the most significant patterns and to draw any useful conclusions. Two formal interviews, with in addition a number of informal contacts with many of the women over a period of two years, produced a formidable body of data.

In the course of the second interview each woman was asked to give information about what had happened to her in the time between the two interviews, and in particular about her relationship with the man who battered her, about her housing situation, the sources of her income, and about the whereabouts and well-being of her children. Faced with the problem of organising data in which time is a crucial dimension, there seemed to be three main ways of presenting the findings: firstly, in terms of what each woman did when she left the refuge, secondly, in terms of her situation at the time of the second interview, and thirdly, in terms of what she did for the majority of the time between the two interviews. Table 4.6 sets out in summary form the woman's relationship with the man who battered her, and her housing situation, firstly, in terms of what she hoped for at the time of the first refuge interview, and then in terms of the three datum points outlined above. The table shows that the women did gradually work towards achieving the aims which they hoped for at the refuge, but it also shows how great were the setbacks which they experienced.

Perhaps the most interesting horizontal lines in Table 4.6 are the second and third; the second shows women hoping to be able to set up new homes for themselves, failing to do so immediately after leaving the refuge, but then working steadily towards their original aim. The third line shows women returning to their husbands after leaving the refuge, even though this was not what they wanted to do, and then gradually making alternative arrangements for themselves and their children.

Relatively little information is available as yet about what happens to women after they have been in refuges. A study of the employment position of women who have been through refuges in South Wales showed that 40 per cent of the women were back with their husbands at the time when the interviews took place; Scottish Women's Aid have suggested, on the basis of statistics collected in refuges, that 41 per cent of women return to their husbands (Welsh Women's Aid, 1980; Scottish Women's Aid, 1980). However, both of these studies were concerned with women who had only recently

Table 4.6: Living arrangements after leaving refuge (in percentages)

N = 42	Hope when at refuge	Destination after refuge	Majority of time between interviews	At second interview
1 In original home, on own	21	21	10	12
2 In new home, on own	60	19	36	43
3 In original home, with husband	10	33	14	9
4 In new home, with husband	2	7	17	12
5 In new home, with new partner	2	2	19	21
6 With friends, relatives, other	5	17	5	2

left refuges. On the basis of my own work, and of that done by the Women's Aid Federation team, I would suggest that it is important to take account of time when discussing this question. Women may indeed return to their husbands, immediately or soon after leaving the refuges, prompted to do so by a great variety of different motives, but the long-term likelihood is that the great majority of these relationships will end in separation or divorce.

The original assumption that women would either return to their husbands, or would live completely separately from them, proved to be an over-simplification. Out of the forty-two women, twenty (48 per cent) never lived with their husbands again after leaving the refuge, while only two lived with their husbands continuously from the time they left the refuge until the time of the second interview. The remaining twenty of the women (48 per cent) made between one and nine attempts at reconciliation, which added up to a total of fifty-one separate reconciliations over the years of the study. Of these only nine couples were still together at the second interview, and, of these, only one woman described her married life in terms which seemed to imply happiness; she was one of the two who returned to her husband after a brief stay at the refuge and remained with him.

This brings us to two central conclusions of the study. Firstly, the evidence suggests that the majority of the women who go to refuges are women whose marriages are ending. About half of the women never returned to their husbands after leaving them to go to the refuge; for the others, the great majority of their attempts at reconciliation failed; only 21 per cent of the women were still with their original partners at the time of the second interview and most of these were unenthusiastic about their married lives. This finding was confirmed by the only similar study, that carried out by the Women's Aid research team: here the proportion of women who were still with their original partner at the time of the second interview was only 11 per cent and the team commented, 'The overall impression is that where women had gone back home, relationships had improved only slightly in most cases and the majority of the women were still very unhappy' (Binney, Harkell and Nixon, 1981).

A second important conclusion is that, though by and large

these marriages are ending, the process of breakdown is typically long and painful. When one remembers that most of the women had experienced violence for some years before coming to the refuge, and when one considers the many attempts at reconciliation which occurred between the two interviews, one is forced to recognise the powerful social and economic forces which work to keep marriages alive and couples together.

Chapter five

Becoming a one-parent family

This chapter describes the lives of the women after they left the refuge and considers especially how they felt about the different possibilities which were open to them. Why did so many make further attempts at reconciliation? Did women keep in touch with their husbands even though they were not living together? What did they like and dislike about life as a single-parent family?

Why, above all, did the women return so often to their husbands? Here again the results of this study are confirmed by the findings of the Women's Aid Federation study (Binney, Harkell and Nixon, 1981). Both studies suggest that the reasons which made women return to their partners *before* they went to the refuge are different from those which made them make attempts at reconciliation *after* the stay at the refuge. Before going to the refuge, when the women first left home, the chief reason for returning to their husbands again was that they had been unable to find satisfactory alternative accommodation; however, after the stay at the refuge, the chief reasons for attempting reconciliation were, firstly, that the women hoped that things would improve, and secondly, that they felt sorry for their husbands. This difference reflects the success of the refuge in helping the most desperate women to find a satisfactory alternative to remaining with their husbands. Women came to the refuge as a last resort, having tried other avenues of escape and found them unsatisfactory; for those who were determined that their marriage should end, the refuge both solved their short-term accommodation problems and gave them time to find long-term solutions to their difficulties.

Many women, however, still faced considerable pressure from husbands who pleaded to be taken back, who promised that the violence would never recur, who clearly loved and were loved by their children, who were inadequately housed themselves and who longed to be back in a proper house. The shortage of accommodation for single people means that many divorced and separated men live in sub-standard accommodation, and when their wives are aware of this they cannot but be touched by it. The following quotations from interview transcripts give some idea of the variety of motives which led women to accept back the men who had assaulted them. Edna was still with her husband at the time of the second interview:

Q. *'Why did you decide to have him back?'*
A. 'More through pity, I think, Jan. I think I more or less pitied him. He'd got nowhere else; his family doesn't really want him; his mum's not in a position to offer him a home – she's living with another of her sons whose marriage has broken down, and I suppose I felt really sorry for him. You've got to have shelter somewhere and being as I knew what it's like to be without, I think this is why I took him back. But we're not really settled; I don't think we ever will be to be honest.'

Q. *'He's not violent any more?'*
A. 'No, he's not so violent now. He often says he's going to do different things, but he doesn't. He drinks an awful lot, Jan, I think this is his main letdown. If he would leave the drink alone, I don't think he'd be nearly so violent as he is. He says to me afterwards, after the little outbursts, "I'm sorry, it were the drink". But the little outbursts are too frequent.'

Q. *'How frequent are they?'*
A. 'Oh, we get it every week; we never go a week without it.'

The following woman was living apart from her husband at the time of the second interview. She and he had been reconciled, and parted again many times.

'So once again, I took him back. You'd think I'd
learn. It was about September when I took him back,
and he said to me, "Marry me." I said, "You're
joking!" And he said to me, "I'm not. I know what's
wrong with me, I'm insecure." And I said to him,
"But you said that, when you wanted the baby, and it
hasn't made any difference. You make so many
promises." And he said to me, "I know it's all
because I'm not married to you. I need you all to be
my family, for me to care for you. I want you to give
up social; I want for me to care for you." So we had a
big white wedding – cost a lot of money – in
October.'

Q. *'And was it different after you were married?'*
A. 'No, in fact, he worsened when I married him. He got
very cocky, and sort of . . . the feeling I got was that
"I've got you, so there you are, I can do what I want".
I *knew* what he was like; I mean someone should get
hold of me and give me a good old slap – because I
knew what he was like. He's ruining my life, and he's
ruining the kids' lives. There was one part of me
saying, "For God's sake, get the kids out!" But there
again, I think, would that be good? I mean is it good
not to have a man behind them? I honestly don't
know; I don't know whether its best for a child to be
without a father, without a proper family; or is it best
to hope and pray that I can change Rodney?'

Some husbands showered their wives with lavish gifts,
sending bunches of red roses, expensive scent, or, in one case,
promising the children new bikes for Christmas if they would
persuade their mother to allow their father, her ex-husband, to
move back in with the family. Some used threats to get what
they wanted. Suzy, whose experiences were described in
chapter 3, said:

'We went to London to my brother's place. Then I got
a phone call from the social worker, saying that he'd
slit his wrist again and she thought that I should go
back to him. And I said, "No, he's done it before, and
its only to get sympathy off people," which it was.

And she said that she thought I was very selfish and that; and she told him where I was.

Q. *'So what happened then?'*

A. 'Well, I couldn't get any help in London, because I wanted a flat in London with the children. I tried the social services and the welfare down there. They said I should come back here. And I said, "Well, the same thing is going to happen again; he's going to threaten me if I come back down here." But they said they couldn't help me down there, so I'd have to come back. [Note: this was some time after the passing of the Housing (Homeless Persons) Act under which she should have been rehoused.] So I came back and I was at my Mum's. And the social worker brought him up with her. He showed the kids his bare arms – because he'd slit his wrists open and that – and he said, "That was your mother's fault." He picked all the stitches out in front of Lisa, and he said, "That's your mother's fault." And then he had to go back into hospital to have it re-stitched, because he picked it in front of Lisa saying that he'd done it because I'd left him.'

Q. *'So where did you stay after that?'*

A. 'Well, the social worker said that if I came back here, she would find me a place to live. And I came back but she never had nowhere for me to go. So I had to go back home. He said he'd go, and he said he wouldn't bother me. But he did, he kept coming back. And then the court ordered us back together again, but in separate bits of the house, which didn't work out. Because he threatened me, about the washing, because I wasn't to do any of his washing, nothing like that, because of going for a divorce – and that caused problems. And he used to time me when I went out – and that caused problems. I had to take him back to court and they gave me an injunction.'

Q. *'What did the injunction say he mustn't do?'*

A. 'Molest me, or come into my bedroom. But of course he was still in the same house.'

Clearly the difficulties which the women faced were by no means over when they left the refuge and many still did not feel settled by the time of the second interview. Claims that 'divorce is too easy nowadays' were not substantiated by this study as it followed the painful and long-drawn-out process of marital breakdown. The 'other' parent's right of access to his or her own child meant that, even when couples were living apart, they were likely to have to meet at intervals. Thus, in addition to the 21 per cent of couples who were still living together, another 21 per cent met at least once a week. Seventeen per cent of the women had completely lost touch with the men who battered them; the remainder of the couples met irregularly. Of the women who were living apart, 17 per cent said that they and their ex-husbands got on quite well together; however, for the majority these meetings were fraught with conflicting emotions. Emma speaks for many of the women in her description of her ex-husband's visits:

> 'He comes in all sort of miserable and weepy and all this. You see, and you've got to switch yourself off, and you've got to sit down and think, "Don't give in and don't feel all sorry; just think of what you went through." That's what I have to do, otherwise I would just be as soft as sugar and just sit there and say, "Oh, well, yes, you might as well come back." '

Q. *'And would you want to live with him again?'*
A. 'No, I wouldn't because I've tasted life on my own now. I know when he comes into this house now, that it's different now. Because, before, when he used to come in drunk and nasty, I was the one that had to run. . . . I mean, he didn't tell me to run, I just ran, because I knew that if I didn't that God knows what would happen. But now, when he comes in to see the children, I can turn round at any time, and say, "Right, well, I'm going to bed now," or, "I've got this to do, can you go?", and he just, as meek as a lamb, gets up and goes out. And that to me, it's a nice feeling, as well as a sad feeling. It's a nice feeling to think that at last, you know, he takes notice of what I say, and it's not me having to run from him.'

Many of the women continued to feel afraid after leaving the refuge, and 31 per cent of them had been subjected to further violence by the men who originally battered them. By contrast, and in response to those who suggest that battered women are masochists who 'attract' violent men, or who 'look for' violent relationships, it might be worth mentioning that none of the women who had made new stable relationships had experienced violence at the hands of their new partners. The happiness of the women who had made new relationships was striking by comparison with the resignation expressed by most of the women who were still living with their original husbands at the time of the second interview.

To sum up, then, it seems that, though the stay at the refuge *was* a turning point for many women, this turning point took many different forms. For about half of the women the refuge provided a way of finally ending an unhappy and dangerous relationship. When they arrived at the refuge some of these women knew exactly what they wanted to do and only needed somewhere to live while an injunction was arranged, divorce proceedings begun and permanent housing secured for them. Other women, however, knew only that they were determined not to return to their husbands but were not clear about how to achieve that end: they needed a great deal of advice and support from workers at the refuge as they set about re-arranging their lives.

The other half of the sample comprised those who were still considering the possibility of reconciliation; about half of these women were back with their husbands at the time of the second interview. For some of this group the stay at the refuge was important in making it clear to husbands that their wives *did* have an alternative to remaining in the matrimonial home, and this in itself could be a deterrent to further violence. For some women the refuge was important in lifting from them a long-standing sense of isolation and shame about having been battered, and in providing them with the help and support which enabled them to make more informed decisions about the alternatives which were open to them. Finally, for very many women the refuge was a place for making friends and creating social networks which remained valuable long after they had left it (Pahl, 1985).

Becoming a one-parent family

All the women were asked a series of questions designed to explore their feelings about being, or becoming, a one-parent family. This seemed an important topic, at a time when there is considerable concern about the increasing numbers of one-parent families; in addition the study provided an unusual opportunity to explore the women's feelings, not after they had made the decision, but over the years when they were considering what to do.

Many studies have documented the difficulties which face most single-parent families, but especially those headed by women (George and Wilding, 1972; Marsden, 1973; Report of the Committee on One Parent Families, 1974; Ferri, 1976; Evason, 1980; Popay et al., 1983). Estimates suggest a total of 890,000 one-parent families in 1980, containing about one and a half million children (Study Commission on the Family, 1983). A much larger number of both adults and children will, of course, pass through a time of being a one-parent family during the course of their lives: these figures are simply the numbers living in one-parent families at any one point in time and as such they underestimate the size of the problem, if it is a problem. One in nine one-parent families is headed by a man, but the great majority are headed by women and it is these families which the research quoted above has identified as facing the greatest difficulties and having the lowest standards of living.

As Evason points out, however, the disadvantaged position of lone mothers and their children is a reflection of the disadvantaged position of women in general. The assumption that women will be the financial dependants of male heads of households has led to a situation in which female wages and conditions of employment make it difficult for them to support a family, and in which women living without a male supporter are still seen as anomalous (Evason, 1980). The problems of the one-parent family derive partly from its lack of a second parent, but substantially from the fact that the one parent is usually female. In addition, it appears that many of the problems faced by the one-parent family arise from the fact that this is still seen as a temporary and regrettable family form; it is almost as though a one-parent family is seen as passing through an unfortunate phase from which, if all goes well, it will in due course be 'rescued' by a second parent and so become a 'real' family. Given the statistics quoted above, one parent families are very much real families in their own right.

The study described here showed that many of the women saw themselves as permanent one-parent families and pointed to advantages as well as as disadvantages: poverty and loneliness were seen as balanced by gains in independence and peace of mind. All the women had had some experience of life as a single parent, if only at the refuge. At the time of the second interview, nine of them were living with their original husbands and nine were living with a new man; twenty-four of the women were living independently, or 'alone'; that is to say they were living neither with the original husband nor with another man. Twenty-one of these women were living with their children as single-parent families; the children of the other three were with their father and the women were living alone or with friends.

Women who had left their children behind when they came to the refuge, or who subsequently lost custody of them to the father, those whose children had grown up and those who had never had children, were all in a particularly difficult position. Though they might be as severely battered as other women they received both less sympathy and less help. They had no right to rehousing under the Housing (Homeless Persons) Act; they often found it impossible to regain possession of the matrimonial home; their morale was often particularly low because they felt that they had failed, not only as wives, but also, and more hurtfully, as mothers. These women are the potential suicides and alcoholics. Few appear in this study because it did not at the outset include women without children – in itself an example of the neglect by researchers of this most vulnerable group of people. The housing needs of single homeless women need urgent consideration, consideration which is beyond the scope of this study.

All the women were asked about living 'alone': this was usually taken to mean living with their children as a single-parent family. The results are set out in Table 5.1. Nearly half of the women said that they liked living alone, or would like

Table 5.1: Women's feelings about living alone as expressed at second interview*

	Women now living as single parent	Women now living with husband	Women now living with new man
Likes living alone or would like it	13	5	1
Dislikes living alone or would dislike it	5	2	7
Don't know/not sure	6	2	1
Total numbers	24	9	9

Note: 'living alone' in most cases means living as a single parent family.

to do so if they could. It is interesting that the proportion saying that they would like to live alone was the same among those currently living alone as it was among those currently living with their original husbands: for both those groups rather more than half said that they would prefer to live alone. The position is very different among those who were living with a new man: here the great majority of the women (seven out of nine) said that they disliked living alone. In some cases it seemed as though this answer reflected happiness in the new relationship; in others, it seemed rather that the making of the new relationship had itself been a response to dislike of living alone.

What was it that women liked and disliked when they gave these answers? As Table 5.2 shows, the aspects of living alone which they particularly liked were the independence, the feeling of being in control of the money and of who came to the house, and the peace of mind which came from not having to live with a violent man. They particularly disliked the loneliness, the boredom and the poverty of life on supplementary benefit. The women spoke eloquently about all these aspects of life in the interviews, but it was perhaps in their letters that the difficulties faced by single-parent families were most clearly expressed. The following are all from letters written between the two interviews. Candy eventually remarried; before that she wrote:

Table 5.2: Feelings about living alone

Aspect of living alone most liked	% of women mentioning each aspect*	Aspect of living alone most disliked	% of women mentioning each aspect*
Independence	55	Loneliness	43
Peace/not living with husband	29	Lack of money	14
Controlling the money	12	Boredom	14
Being able to have friends in	10	Worries about children	7
Nothing	10	Nothing	21

*Percentages may add up to more than 100 because of women giving more than one answer.

Since I left the refuge nothing has gone right. I have had boyfriends, but then have been rejected. As soon as they have been told that I have a daughter they haven't wanted to see me any more. I just don't know what to do. I'm living with my friend's family at the moment. Before that I was in my own flat, but I felt so lonely and depressed so I gave it up. . . . I've even thought of going back to my husband but I thought about it quite strongly, and I know that it wouldn't be worth it, as he'll only be like he was before, battering Donna and I about and that is no life for her or myself. It'll only mean more unhappiness for Donna and I, and I think I've had my share of loneliness and being unhappy.

Lena was living alone throughout the time of the study, and found it hard. She wrote:

I find life very lonely and people tend to leave you out of things when there is no man around. Also there is not enough being done for one-parent families, even social workers are a let-down. We are lucky compared with

others, in as much as we have each other and we have
security, but of course poverty is a big hold back.

Paula went back to her husband, was savagely beaten over
many months, and eventually left him for good. She wrote:

> Thank you for your letter. It's nice to know someone
> cares enough to want to know how we are keeping and
> coping on our own. You get to feel no one gives a damn
> how you feel, or how you manage to feed and clothe
> yourself and children.
>
> When we went home that June I hoped that Mark and I
> would finally get ourselves sorted out, but as usual we
> were splitting up, then getting back together again, and
> each time the violence got worse. Things cane to a head
> on Easter weekend, from Friday evening it was beatings
> after beatings, I had a lovely black eye for my Easter
> egg . . . [so she moved to a new town to escape]. I've
> found one of the difficulties of moving into a new town
> is you don't know anyone and neighbours don't want to
> get too involved when they learn you haven't a husband.
> All I had was a bed, three-piece suite, one carpet and a
> table. I didn't have a cooker till two weeks after. It was so
> lonely in the empty house. The social security sent me
> £100 to buy saucepans and sheets. I still live in fear of
> Mark, he is always there at the back of my mind. I'm
> afraid to go to bed at night, I lie awake listening to every
> sound, I suppose it's just a habit I've got into over the
> years. Some days I feel no one gives a damn whether we
> wake up or not, and other days I feel quite pleased with
> myself, to have made a new home and life for myself and
> the boys. I've been going to the furniture auctions these
> last few weeks and the house is now starting to look like
> a home at last. I have been making myself a little short of
> money, but it was worth while to see it looking more like
> a home.

Doris, who never returned to her husband after the refuge, was
more cheerful. She wrote:

> Please forgive the rotten writing. I am indulging in my
> freedom, writing to you and listening to piano concertos.
> I am so relaxed and happy. I hardly ever go out. I keep

67

my brain active with books about my own court cases
and the cause of battered wives. The officer of the DHSS
called today; he was very charming, but he made a fatal
mistake. He said the children were a handicap to me.
Although it's true without them my life would have
different choices – I still feel freedom with them. It's
marvellous to make my own decisions and not fear
violent repercussions.

Thus by the time of the second interview many of the
women saw being a single-parent family not as a negative but
as a positive state. They did not feel that they had lost
something, but rather that they had gained in strength, in
confidence and in control over their lives. This is perhaps an
appropriate point at which to suggest that there was no one
'right' solution to the women's problems. 'Good' solutions
seemed to have been achieved by women who returned to
their husbands, by those who had made new relationships,
and by those living as single-parent families; 'bad' solutions,
giving rise to unhappiness for both adults and children, were
similarly found among all three groups of women.

Sources of income

A major difficulty facing women after leaving the refuge was
that of finding a satisfactory source of income for themselves
and their children. Table 5.3 shows patterns of income
maintenance at the time of the second interview: it is striking
that maintenance paid by ex-husbands was negligible as a
source of support by comparison with social security and
earnings.

All forty-two of the women turned to social security for help
at some time or other during the years covered by the study.
By definition a woman claimed in her own right only as a
single-parent family: when living with her husband it would
be he who claimed. The social security was the agency to
which women turned more than any other; it was seen as the
most helpful of all agencies when the women were interviewed at the refuge but the *least* helpful of all at the time of
the second interview. (Seventy-six per cent of women

described social security as helpful at the first interview, compared with 43 per cent at the second.) This difference seems to reflect both the changing circumstances of the women and their changing needs; it may also reflect differences between offices.

Table 5.3: Sources of income at time of second interview

	women living independently	women with husband	women with new partner	% of total (n = 42)
Social security	15	2		41
Earnings	2	7	9	43
Social security + maintenance	4			10
Social security + earnings	2			4
Other	1			
Total numbers	24	9	9	100

When women first arrived at the refuge it seemed as though they saw social security as helpful partly because their expectations were so low. Some arrived at the refuge unaware of the fact that they would be able to claim supplementary benefit for themselves and their children: indeed, some had stayed with their husbands because they could see no way of supporting themselves financially away from them. Though women were often affronted by what they perceived as impertinent questioning, and exhausted by long waits in social security offices, they were nevertheless grateful that some financial help was available. As we have seen, some women even commented that they were better off living on supplementary benefit than they had been when living with their husbands.

By the time of the second interview, however, most of the women had had considerable experience of life on supplementary benefit. They knew more about the correct rates and about the exceptional needs payments which they, or people known to them, had received in the past. Many felt that they knew more about the rights of claimants than did the counter clerks. In addition, those women who were still living on supplementary benefit had by this time spent two or three years living on an extremely low income. They were becoming very weary both of the humiliations of being a claimant and of the hardships of life in poverty. At the time of the second interview 41 per cent of the women in the study were living entirely on supplementary benefit; the great majority of these were women living alone and bringing up young children. Another 14 per cent were receiving income from earnings or from maintenance payments but were receiving supplementary benefit in order to raise their income to the scale rates.

Perhaps more importantly, as far as attitudes to social security were concerned, most of the women had faced and overcome the problem involved in setting up a new home on a pitifully small income. Time and time again I carried out follow-up interviews in comfortable, pleasant homes and heard how the furnishings had been painstakingly acquired from secondhand shops or auctions, or given by friends and relations. The majority of the women (67 per cent) had at some time or other received exceptional needs payments. However, in general these payments were quite small and only four of the women reported receiving sums of over £100. I never ceased to be impressed by the skill, determination and ingenuity which so many of the women had shown in building up homes with such limited resources. The sums allowed for floor coverings, furniture or kitchen equipment seemed to underestimate greatly the real costs of such items, even if bought secondhand.

There were three main problems related to social security. The first of these was the question of how much the women were entitled to receive.

The most common criticism made by women was of errors in payments or of the failure of social security officials to explain how payments were calculated or what other benefits were available. Several women commented that once they themselves had learnt what they were entitled to receive their relationships with their local supplementary benefit office improved. As Doris said,

'I think in the beginning you have to fight like hell to
get what you are entitled to. But I think that from
then on, if you are fair with them, I think that they
will be fair with you.'

Q. *'Have you ever had exceptional needs payments?'*
A. 'Only for the children's clothes. They've always come
and they've always moaned and complained a bit.
But I've said, "Well look, the little girl wets the bed
every night, and I do all my own washing, and I have
to replace this, that and the other." And they've
always been very good then – they are only small
sums, something like eighteen quid, which for three
kids isn't much. But I trot along to the secondhand
shop and it helped.'

Women very much appreciated those social security officials
who took the trouble to explain the scale rates and the system
of entitlements. Amy described how:

'They came round and saw me and they told me what I
was entitled to. They did tell me everything. And when I
did send for a clothes allowance, they did send me
everything that I asked for, and I was quite surprised that
the prices were up-to-date.'

These interviews were all carried out before the reform of the
supplementary benefit system in November 1980; the aim of
the reform is to simplify the system and to reduce the area of
discretion. This study would suggest that it is important to
combine these reforms with a real attempt to explain to
claimants both the basis upon which decisions are made and
the range of benefits to which they might be entitled. Such
explanations not only reduce the uncertainty and humiliation
involved in claiming, but also make for a more efficient
service. Lacking such explanations from the social security
office, claimants have to rely upon alternative sources of
information. For the women in this study the refuge was an
important source of information about social security: this
suggests that all refuges should provide information, not just
about the benefits to which women are entitled while at the

refuge, but also about benefits to which they may become entitled when they leave.

A second problem concerned the relationship between payments made by social security offices and those made by husbands. Some offices still put considerable pressure on women in an attempt to get maintenance from husbands. Having seen how often disputes over money had occurred in these marriages it is perhaps not surprising that so few of these attempts were successful. Only four of the twenty-four women who were living independently at the time of the second interview had succeeded in getting maintenance, and for none of these did it provide an adequate income; all the women had to claim supplementary benefit in addition to their maintenance.

A third problem for many women concerned getting paid employment and so ending their dependence on supplementary benefit. An important finding is that *all* the women who were living as single parents on supplementary benefit would have preferred to have been in paid employment. The overwhelming reason for not taking employment was responsibility for child care. This finding would suggest that an expansion in community provision for child care would reduce the numbers of families dependent on supplementary benefit. Women whose children were old enough, or who had found alternative ways of caring for them, seemed to take jobs as soon as they could and seemed also to be willing to do unpleasant and low-paid work in order to avoid what they saw as the humiliation of dependence on the state. As Sarah said:

'I claimed social (security) for a few weeks, but I was lucky and I got out on the potatoes and I stopped my claim right away. That was worse than anything – and all for £14. The rent was £4 and that left £10 to feed three of us. Oh, no!'

Many women with small children found themselves caught in what could best be described as a three-sided trap. On the first side of this trap was the husband, unreliable both in the amount he earned and in the amount he gave his wife for housekeeping; on the second side was the social security, more reliable perhaps, but resented for its invasion of privacy and for the meagreness of its payments; and on the third side was the possibility of paid employment, made impossible by the demands of children and the lack of child care facilities. Sally described this dilemma as she experienced it; she has three children, the youngest of whom is a baby, and at the time of her second interview she had left her husband in yet another attempt to build an independent life.

'I've been trying, since I've been here, to get a job. You see the problem is, is her. I went for an interview the other day. I got the job but it's the baby. I could have got £35 wages, put in for FIS . . . family . . . you know, for one-parent families. I would have been a lot better off, but as I said, who's going to have the baby and who's going to have the kids when they're on holidays. To be quite honest, I can't get a job till the bab goes to school and that's the long and short of it.

'You see social think that you just want to scrounge all the time, off of them. But that's not true, because you have women like me, couldn't give a damn for social – they want to go out (to work). They don't want to have to go up there and tell them all their private business, because they want to know the ins and outs, they really do.

'I'm sure they think we're fiddling now. Because when he was sick he never had a doctor's certificate. I went up there and I said, "Look, he hasn't got a doctor's note, but he also hasn't got no wages. So give me enough money to feed me and the kids." "No, we can't; because you're living with him." So I said, "Well, if that's the only way I can get some money, then I'll leave him." And then, of course, vroom, two weeks later, but I did leave him. It had nothing to do with it: it was because I found out what he'd been doing. But to be truthful, I would have done it, Jan, because that's the only way I would have had, I would have had to leave him to feed my kids because I wasn't getting a penny from him.'

With an estimated 890,000 one-parent families in Britain in 1980, over 60 per cent of them headed by a divorced or separated mother, the three-cornered trap keeps many women and their children in poverty (Study Commission on the Family, 1983).

Chapter six

The search for help

In this final chapter of Part I we turn to consider the help which the women sought for their difficulties. Here we shall be concerned both with the time before the women went to the refuge and with the time after they left it. The aim of this chapter will be to set the scene for Part II, in which we will consider in more detail the ways in which different agencies can help abused women.

It is important to remember that this study focused on the women who went to one refuge. By comparison with abused women in the general population, the refuge users probably had a number of characteristics in common. Until further research is carried out, however, it is impossible to do more than hypothesise about these differences. We cannot be sure whether women who go to refuges are more desperate, or simply better informed, than those who do not; nor can we say whether they are less resourceful in that they have been unable to find alternative sources of help, or more resourceful in that they have been brave enough to take the very drastic step of leaving home with their children to go to an unknown institution, often in an unknown town. It is clear, however, that abused women who go to refuges are a minority of those who turn to public agencies for help, who are probably themselves a minority of all those wives whose husbands assault and abuse them.

The number of women who are assaulted by the men with whom they live greatly exceeds the number using refuges or local authority homeless family accommodation. Estimates of the size of the overall problem are notoriously inadequate: the position in Britain was summed up by Marsden:

> [Evidence from studies of divorce] would indicate an incidence of about 5%. Other evidence seems to place the incidence of violent marriages at between 1% and 5%, of rarely violent marriages at up to 15% and the remainder of non-violent marriages at around 80%. (Marsden, 1978, 125)

Even if we take the very lowest of all these estimates, 1 per cent of all marriages in Britain produces a total for 1981 of over 128,000 violent marriages (Central Statistical Office, 1983). Evidence drawn from police records suggests that in the great majority of these marriages the husband will be the violent partner (Dobash and Dobash, 1980, 20).

Few agencies keep the sort of records from which it is possible to calculate the numbers of abused women who contact public agencies. It has often been suggested that police records, for example, should differentiate incidents of wife assault from 'domestic disputes', and that social service departments should keep records distinguishing wife abuse from other family problems, but neither of these have so far been put into effect on any but a local basis. The exceptions to this are housing departments' records of people accepted into homeless family accommodation, and, of course, refuges for battered women. In 1978 there were about 200 refuges in England and Wales, which provided places for 11,400 women during the year from September 1977 to September 1978 (Binney, Harkell and Nixon, 1981); there are also about twenty-five refuges in Scotland, which in the year 1979-80 accommodated 800 women and 1,470 children (Scottish Women's Aid, 1980; Convention of Scottish Local Authorities, 1980). A smaller number of abused women are accommodated in homeless family accommodation provided by housing departments. In the first half of 1978, 2,900 people were accepted into homeless family accommodation because of violent marital disputes: this would suggest a total of perhaps 6,000 for the whole year. Any calculations in this most difficult area must be treated with extreme scepticism. However, adding the number of women who used the refuges to the number of those who entered homeless family accommodation because of violence, one reaches a total of

18,200 women, a total which is certainly an underestimate because some women will have paid more than one visit to refuges. This number is far below the total of 128,000 which as we have seen is the *lowest* possible estimate of the total number of marriages in which violence occurs.

However, though we know little about the majority of battered women, studies based on interviews with women at refuges show consistent patterns of help seeking. For most the first reaction is one of shame and a sense of failure. As Marilyn said, talking of violence which had lasted since her marriage began fifteen years before:

> 'He'd just get me in a chair and stand there lecturing me, I timed him once, three hours, on and on, just lecturing – how fantastic he was and how terrible I was, and that I should put up with it, everybody else's wife put up with it. And in the end I started to believe it. I thought, that's what being married is. I had a poker thrown at me – just because his tea was too weak – he just takes it for granted, if you're married you'll have to accept it. It's part of being a wife.'

Like many others, Marilyn had been too ashamed at first to be able to talk to anyone else about the violence. The first people in whom she confided were her mother and her best friend; she left home five times before going to the refuge, always going to her friend, but never being able to stay for more than a few days because her husband knew where he would find her and was always able to persuade her to return home by threats of violence or promises of reform.

Asked about more formal sources of help, Marilyn's answers reflected the complexities of her own and other people's ideas about privacy, as well as feelings of shame and fear; it is this complex web of constraints that continues to trap abused women within their homes and marriages:

Q. *'Did you ever call the police in?'*
A. 'No. No! I was just terrified to do anything really, you know. Sounds silly to be so frightened of somebody, but I was. Oh, no.'

Q. *'What about your neighbour: was she helpful?'*
A. 'Not really. A few times people have said, "Oh, we

nearly called the police last night because we could
hear screams or something." But people, you know
what people are like, they don't want to get involved
really.'

Q. *'What about going to a social worker?'*
A. 'I was just too frightened to tell anybody, because if I
had he'd have gone mad again. And you don't like to
admit that sort of thing to somebody else. You think
they'll think, "Oh, failure there!" You feel you must
have gone wrong somewhere for it to be like that.'

Many wives put up with the violence for years without
confiding in anyone, in order to protect both their husbands'
pride and their own marriages. The idea that an unhappy
marriage must necessarily be a 'failure' is a pervasive one. As
Alison said of her Indian husband's family:'

'You see, you can't say nothing to them. He's very proud.
If I was to tell them half of what goes on they'd disown
him and I wouldn't like it. I mean, I'm not a wicked
person. He says I am, but I'm not. I think to myself, if
anything happened between me and him, and I do leave
him, and I take the children, what's his mum going to
think?'

Many wives even went to the length of lying to save their
husband's face, as Emma did when her engineer husband
threw her downstairs after hitting her about the head:

'The nurse came up to me and said, "Come in, Emma,
let's have a look." I took my hand away from my head
and the blood all went "whoosh". So she said, "What
happened? How have you done that?" So I said, "Oh
don't laugh – I fell over one of the children's toys and cut
myself." She just said, "Oh yes." And then I went into
the surgeon to have him stitch it and he said, "I know
what that is. Somebody's hit you, on your mouth." And I
said, "No, I fell over." "But you haven't," he said. He
didn't bother to keep asking me; just stitched it up and
we came home.'

In the end, however, Emma finally decided that the time had
come to leave her husband:

'At night time, when I used to stand outside, or in the greenhouse, I used to think to myself, "What am I doing out here?" Everybody else asleep in bed, normally, and there's me so petrified to go in the house, because of him. I thought, "I can't see the Prime Minister coming out of her house at three o'clock in the morning and spending the night in the bushes, just so that her husband can get some sleep, or because he's drunk." Something clicked. That's how I felt on my birthday. I couldn't take any more.'

It is important to remember that it is to their family and friends that most people, including battered women, turn first for help: it is only when these informal sources of help prove inadequate that people turn to officials and organisations. The amount of 'welfare' provided by the agencies of the welfare state is far less than that provided by the family, usually by its female members (Finch and Groves, 1983). It seems likely that the great majority of battered women either put up with the violence, or find some solution to their problems without seeking the help of any professional, except that of the solicitor who handles their divorce. It does seem that the longer violence continues the more likely it is that professionals, such as general practitioners, social workers, health visitors, housing managers or members of the legal profession are likely to be involved. As Dobash, Dobash and Cavanagh say, 'as the violence persisted [women] continued to use informal sources quite heavily but increasingly approached formal sources, particularly doctors, social workers and the police' (this volume, page 150).

Three-quarters of the women had turned to relatives, usually mothers and sisters, for help, and rather more than half of the siblings and rather less than half of the parents were seen as 'helpful', as Table 6.1 shows. More striking, however, is the very great importance of friends as sources of help, especially after the women had left the refuge. This was the time when women were facing the problems of setting up a new home and adjusting to life as a one-parent family. Some of these friendships had been maintained for many years; but many had been made at the refuge and others were new relationships made through organisations such as Gingerbread. The great majority of these friends were women, very often single parents in a similar position who could share some of the worries and hardships of bringing up children alone. One important finding of the study is the great value of meeting places for single parents, such as Gingerbread, women's refuges, and women's centres, and the need for more such organisations.

Table 6.1: Individuals and agencies consulted by the women and the extent to which they were helpful (N = 42)

	Before the refuge		After the refuge	
	% of women who asked for help	% of those contacted who were helpful	% of women who asked for help	% of those contacted who were helpful
Parents	74	49	74	48
Siblings	76	59	88	54
Friends/neighbours	67	75	95	93
Doctor	62	42		
Police	71	37	50	81
Social workers	76	56	74	74
Health visitors	29	58	53	64
Social security	93	76	100	43
Solicitors	60	76	81	76
Housing dept.			83	57

About half of the women were relatively isolated socially before going to the refuge: 24 per cent said that they had no relative or friend to whom they could go for help, while another 29 per cent had only one such helper. There seemed to be three main reasons for this isolation: some women were isolated by their feelings of shame and by a desire to protect their husbands from the disapproval of others; some were isolated by mobility, either because they had come to Britain from another country or because they had recently moved house within Britain; and, finally, some were isolated because their links with kin had been broken by family quarrels, or by death or divorce.

This study suggests that one characteristic which distinguishes battered women who go to refuges from women in the general population who are battered is that a substantial minority of the former lack close relatives. At the time of the first interview 35 per cent of the women either had no mother living, or if she was still alive, had not seen her for more than a year; more strikingly, 67 per cent of the women either had no father living, or had not seen him for more than a year. These figures reflect the fact that 43 per cent of the women's parents' marriages had already ended in the death of one partner, while another 24 per cent had ended in divorce. Other studies have documented the processes by which marital problems and marital breakdown are themselves associated with the breaking of links with kin, so that help may be least available just when it is most needed (Marsden, 1973; Marris, 1958). The study described here suggests another dimension to the question of the relationship between a couple and members of their extended families: this is that, for couples with rather few kin links, the process of marital breakdown can be particularly painful and protracted. Such couples may be more dependent than most on the services provided by the agencies of the welfare state.

Before coming to the refuge many women were isolated by what they saw as 'their' failure to have a successful marriage. Battered women share the commonly held fallacy that they are to blame for the violence, that they in some way caused it to happen. These feelings affected most of the women, but were perhaps particularly strong among the more outwardly respectable. Though few middle-class women actually stayed at the refuge, they were over-represented among women who were advised by refuge workers over the telephone, and among those who asked for discreet visits to be paid by the workers to their homes. The problem of shame was described by Doris:

> 'A "battered wife" to me was definitely low working class . . . low mentality . . . hundreds of kids . . . probably with an Irish accent . . . he came home from the pub, probably bashed her up and down the path outside, before he bashed her all round the house indoors. None of that was present – so therefore, I

wasn't a "battered wife". I remember I phoned the refuge; I said, "I'm not sure if I am a battered wife, I've got a black eye, but I don't think I'm a battered wife." She said, "Why not?" I said, "Well, because I've got plenty of money, and a big car."

Q. And did you find it hard to say, "I am a battered wife"?

A. No, I found it a tremendous relief – because I could stop blaming myself. It used to depress me thinking that I was a bit peculiar – you were the only person whose husband knocked you about; you were a failure, and your judgment ought to be better. I no longer had to be ashamed.'

There were some clear differences between the help which the women sought before and after their stay at the refuge. In the report on the first part of the study their needs on arrival at the refuge were seen as fourfold: protection, accommodation, advice and support (Pahl, 1978). That is to say, at that time the women were chiefly concerned with removing themselves and their children from the violence, with getting advice as to what courses of action were open to them, and with receiving support while they decided what to do.

After they left the refuge, however, women tended to be concerned with starting a new life, with the welfare of their children, with finding a decent house and making it comfortable, and with adapting to whatever relationship continued between themselves and the man who battered them. For about a third of them the relationship with this man was a source of continuing anxiety: for these women the need for protection continued to be extremely important. However, for the women as a whole their needs were now more similar to those of most one-parent families; that is to say, they needed help with child care, an adequate house and a reasonable income.

It must be recognised that a drawback of this study is that we have only the women's accounts of the difficulties which they faced, and of the responses of those to whom they went for help. For example, each woman was asked whether she had seen a social worker, what she had hoped would be done for her, what the response of the social worker had been and whether that response had been helpful. In all of this the woman's definition of what happened is paramount. Sometimes it is clear from the women's answers that the social worker, or other professional, had adopted a different definition of the situation; when this happened the professional was often defined as 'unhelpful', though sometimes excuses were made by the women for those who had been unable, rather than unwilling, to see the problem in its full complexity. As one woman said of her social worker: 'He wasn't very helpful really; it was all a bit much for him, I think; he was very young.'

Few studies of the helping professions have overcome the problem of the different ways in which different people may describe the same incident. Numerous studies have explored how doctors, social workers, social security officials and so on see their roles; rather fewer studies have been concerned with what patients, clients, claimants and others feel about their side of the story. However, studies which analyse what each side felt about the *same* meeting are very rare indeed. Those few studies which have drawn together two accounts of the same event, especially when that event is someone trying to get help from an agent of the welfare state, show that there are often enormous discrepancies between the accounts of the event given by the two participants. As Stuart Rees said in his study of clients and their social workers:

> The development of the mismatch in client/social worker perspectives on 'service required' can be illustrated in the controversy over client's eligibility for help and in client's confusion about social workers' proposed and actual remedies. There is a common factor in both situations. The client does not seem to be aware that he is involved in a bargaining transaction, the social worker fails to make it explicit that the agenda for meetings can be shared, that decisions are open to negotiation. (Rees, 1974, 267; see also Rees, 1978)

However, even though we do not know what account the agents of the welfare state would have given of their meetings with the women, I would argue that the women's accounts are valid in themselves. Their subjective interpretations, both of their needs and of the solutions which were offered to them, were crucial in shaping the decisions which they made on behalf of themselves and their children.

The question of 'need' is a complicated one, which has been widely discussed elsewhere. Need may be measured in absolute or comparative terms, may be defined objectively or subjectively. The definition adopted here is necessarily a subjective one, equating need with what Bradshaw called 'felt need' (Bradshaw, 1972; see also Forder, 1974; Shaw, 1974; Culyer, 1976). There are limitations with this definition since it means that 'need' is circumscribed by the knowledge and expectations of the needy person, who may be unrealistically optimistic or pessimistic. However, the strength of the definition is the primacy it gives to the experience of the client/patient/claimant, as opposed to the possibly contradictory definitions of the situation adopted by more powerful individuals. Differences in the women's own definition of their needs before and after their stay at the refuge are reflected in their evaluation of the help which they received. Characteristically, the women turned to informal sources of help before formal sources of help, and sought solutions which would enable them to stay in their own homes before accepting solutions which involved them in leaving home. Thus, going to a refuge or to homeless family accommodation was very much a last resort. Table 6.1 sets out the women's answers to the questions about the help which they had sought and about the helpfulness of the responses which they had encountered. Women were asked whether each particular individual or agency was 'helpful', 'quite helpful' or 'not helpful', and the first two of these were combined to produce the category of 'helpful'.

Before coming to the refuge more than half of the women had contacted one or more of the following about their problems: their general practitioner, the police and the social services. Fewer than half of the general practitioners and of the police had proved helpful; rather over half of the social workers were described as helpful, often because it was the social worker who had been responsible for the woman's arrival at the refuge. During their first week at the refuge, that is before the first interview, many of the women had contacted solicitors and the great majority had been to the social security office to claim supplementary benefit. Satisfaction with these two agencies was much greater, both being described as 'helpful' by 76 per cent of the women. Other sources of help, in order of the extent to which they were contacted and found helpful, were Citizens' Advice Bureaux, the Samaritans, Gingerbread, the Marriage Guidance Council, the churches and the National Society for the Prevention of Cruelty to Children.

After the stay at the refuge women continued to need help, though this need diminished as the months went by. More than half of the women had contacted one or more of the following about their problems: a social worker, a health visitor, the social security, a solicitor and the housing department. Exactly half of the women had had to call in the police at some time or other after leaving the refuge. Interestingly, the police were now described as one of the most helpful of the official agencies. Solicitors continued to be seen as helpful after leaving the refuge, while social workers and health visitors rose in the women's estimation. The agency which was seen as least helpful, and which fell most in the women's estimation, was the social security office. Let us briefly consider what it was that the women were looking for when they asked for help and what were seen as helpful or unhelpful responses on the part of agencies.

In general, helpfulness on the part of statutory agencies was seen in terms of providing relevant and accurate information, accepting the woman's own definition of the problem, and providing practical help and continuing support while a solution was being sought. For many women the most important piece of information was the fact that they could claim supplementary benefit in their own right if they were living separately from their husbands. It is also important that all those who come into contact with battered women are familiar with the whereabouts of the nearest women's refuge, and that they are aware of the provisions of the Housing (Homeless Persons) Act and of the Matrimonial Proceedings and Domestic Violence Act. It is important that battered women are not continually referred on to yet another agency; perhaps the essence of the problem is that, because it is potentially the concern of so many people, it can easily become the concern of nobody – except of the woman herself.

More specific forms of help can be offered by members of

different professions. General practitioners who were seen as 'helpful' had many characteristics in common. The women described how these doctors listened carefully, approached the problem sympathetically and offered appropriate advice, both medical and non-medical. One of the women who was most enthusiastic about the helpfulness of her general practitioner described how he frequently arranged for her to have the last appointment of the surgery so that there should be plenty of time to discuss her difficulties. General practitioners could also be extremely useful in the long term by making careful records, on the woman's first visit, about the nature and extent of her injuries. These records became important when evidence about the violence was needed, either for a court of law or as evidence to a housing department of the woman's right to assistance under the Housing (Homeless Persons) Act. Lacking such medical records, some women were advised, in effect, to go home, get beaten again and then present themselves with the evidence of abuse. Women also appreciated those doctors who were concerned, not just with the injuries, but with the whole range of problems each individual faced. Because of their physical injuries abused women will continue to go to general practitioners for help; yet without considering the problem in its context, and without being aware of a wide range of non-medical solutions, several practitioners can give only limited help (Pahl, 1979b; Women's Aid Federation (England), 1980a).

Helpfulness on the part of social workers was seen differently at the first, as opposed to the second, interview. At the first interview, when women had recently arrived at the refuge, helpfulness was seen in terms of getting advice, of finding accommodation, and, in particular, of advising women about the existence of the refuge. Social workers were an important source of advice over a wide range of different areas, from housing to income maintenance to the law, and the most helpful social workers were those who were able to give women accurate and relevant information about the questions which were troubling them. In particular, before going to the refuge, information about accommodation was valued and transport from the matrimonial home to the refuge. Social services departments were the most frequently cited source of referrals to the refuge, with one-third of the women mentioning social workers as the people who told them of its existence. Many of these social workers took women and their children to the refuge by car. This was important because, for a woman with several children and little or no money, with clothes for an indefinitely long stay crammed into suitcases or plastic dustbin bags, simply leaving home can present insuperable obstacles.

At the second interview the women talked of the help which they had received from social workers after leaving the refuge. By that time the emphasis was different, with most of the women being concerned about making a new home and about the problems of life as a single-parent family. At this stage helpfulness was seen in terms of negotiating over housing, finding ways of obtaining furniture and kitchen equipment, and making arrangements for child care. The help given to the women by social workers included negotiating with local authority housing departments, over both the allocation and the repair of houses, obtaining beds and bedding, furniture and cookers, arranging care for children in play groups and day nurseries, in local authority children's homes and with foster parents. Some social services departments appeared to function as efficient 'resource centres' collecting and distributing a wide range of 'goods': such 'resource centres' can provide social workers with the means to offer the very tangible help which many studies, including this one, show to be particularly valued by clients. Above all, perhaps, the women valued social workers for their ability to 'work the system' on their behalf: this meant knowing who to write to about a leaking roof, how to get a council house tenancy transferred from husband to wife and what office to apply to for free school dinners or a uniform grant; it meant knowing about the provisions of the Housing (Homeless Persons) Act, the Domestic Violence and Matrimonial Proceedings Act, and a range of other legislation relating to housing, divorce and income maintenance; and it meant applying this knowledge to the particular circumstances of one woman and one family. A social worker who can do all this can provide invaluable help.

Health visitors were an under-used source of assistance: a few were extremely helpful but most were seen by the women as interested only in the welfare of the children. Since battering so often begins, or intensifies, when a woman is pregnant or has young children, and since this is the time when health visitors call routinely, it would seem that they could play a crucial role in helping women who are assaulted by the men with whom they live.

When health visitors were described as helpful it was normally because they had made an effort to understand the woman's position as she saw it, and because they had responded in a way which was seen as appropriate. One of the most helpful health visitors learnt not to call at the house when the husband's van was parked outside: her visits were all made when the husband was out.

The fact that health visitors are seen as concerned mainly with young children has both advantages and disadvantages. It can be an advantage in that it provides an acceptable reason for a woman to talk to someone from 'the welfare'. It is very difficult for a wife to take the drastic and positive step of going to see a social worker, a step which she herself may see as an acknowledgment of her personal failure, and which her husband may see as a threat to himself and to the family. By contrast the routine visit of the uninvited health visitor can provide an opportunity to discuss other problems under cover of discussing the children's health. On the other hand, it has grave disadvantages in that, once again, it appears that the needs of the woman are subsumed under those of the children. Many women commented that they did not see the health visitor as an appropriate person to talk to about the husband's violence because her interest and responsibility lay with the children. Yet is is clear that the responsibility of health visitors, in theory at least, does extend to the health of all members of the community within which they work (Council for the Education and Training of Health Visitors, 1977; Owen, 1977; Pahl, 1982b).

At the first interview it appeared that the willingness of the police to help reflected not just the extent of the woman's injuries, but also the marital status and housing position of the couple. The results suggested that the police were less likely to be seen as helpful when the woman was living with the man who assaulted her, and was married to him. They were more likely to be seen as helpful when the couple either were living together but were not married, or were married but were not living together. These results reflect the comments of the women that the police were often reluctant to intervene between husband and wife and unwilling to enter a private home unless invited to do so by the 'head' of the household (Pahl, 1982a).

After the stay at the refuge, however, the position with regard to the police changed. Twenty-one of the women had had to call on the police for help between the time of leaving the refuge and the time of the second interview. Usually this was in order to give protection during an attempt at reconciliation, or to enforce an injunction against a husband who persisted in pestering his wife. The answers at the second interview showed that the police now appeared as one of the most helpful agencies, with 77 per cent of those who called on them reporting that they had been helped. It seems that this reflects the changed definition of the situation by the officers called to these cases, particularly when an injunction was in force. In theory, neither the police nor the criminal law discriminate either between assaults taking place in or outside of the home, or between an assault by a spouse as opposed to by a stranger. However, the evidence of this study suggests that married women who are assaulted by their husbands are *less* likely than other victims of assault to receive effective help from the police.

Of the forty-two women, seventeen had obtained injunctions against their husbands during or after their stay at the refuge, eight of these having a power of arrest attached. One other woman was still waiting for an injunction at the time of the second interview. Of the seventeen women with injunctions in force, five said that the injunction had proved ineffective in protecting them against their husbands. However, the majority of the women said either that the injunction had proved an effective measure, or that its existence had been enough to prevent further violence. Injunctions seemed to serve three main functions: they indicated unequivocally to husbands that violent behaviour towards wives is not acceptable; they served to label the women as people whose complaints to the police ought to be taken seriously; and they gave an effective remedy to the police if violence recurred. (See also Ansell, 1978; Migdall, 1980.)

When women described the failure of agencies to help,

there were a number of common threads running through their accounts. Firstly, there were many cases in which agencies simply failed to offer the help they might have been expected to provide. Into this category came the policeman who said, 'We're not allowed to get involved', the general practitioner who said, 'What do you think this is, a bloody marriage guidance bureau', the social workers who gave no advice on welfare rights and the housing departments who found ways to evade all responsibility for rehousing women with children. Even when women were rehoused it seemed as if they were given the most dilapidated housing, while better accommodation went to families with two parents. This finding is supported by the results of the Women's Aid research which highlighted the poor quality of the housing offered to women (Binney, Harkell and Nixon, this volume). Thus for many women there appeared to have been a very big gap between the help that was in theory available and the help they received in practice. This gap was apparent in all areas, but was particularly evident when considering sources of help which had been covered by statutory legislation (See also Parker, this volume.)

Secondly, there was a tendency for agencies to blame the women for the couples' marital problems. Sometimes this took the form of suggestions that women should 'try again', or 'go back and make it up'. More drastically, it took the form of reference to a psychiatrist: it is interesting that other researchers have also found evidence of abused women being referred to psychiatrists and mental hospitals (Dobash and Dobash, 1980; Maynard, this volume). Referral to a psychiatrist would seem to be a clear instance of 'blaming the victim' (Ryan, 1971). The women felt more ambivalent, however, about the suggestion that they should spend some time in a psychiatric hospital as one way of temporarily escaping from their problem. On the one hand a stay in a psychiatric hospital would seem to imply that it is the woman, and not her husband, who is the problem. By treating her as though it is her depression, her stress and her suicide attempts which are the problem, rather than seeing these symptoms as consequences of the violence of her husband, responsibility for the whole problem is shifted on to her shoulders. Stark et al. have documented the process by which the American medical profession exacerbates the problem of battered women by ignoring the battering and treating the complaints associated with abuse symptomatically. They found that a high proportion of women attempting suicide had been battered shortly before their attempt; ironically they also found that battered women were more likely than non-battered women to be labelled as 'hysterical' or 'inadequate' and were more likely to be sent home early and without any in-patient care (Stark *et al.*, 1979).

On the other hand, a few women felt that a stay in a psychiatric hospital gave them some respite from the violence and a chance to think what they should do. Four women described how they had been admitted to psychiatric hospitals 'for a rest'; however, since it was acknowledged by the hospital staff that they were not ill in any way, they were only allowed to stay in for two or three weeks. Some had used hospitals in rather the same way that women used the refuge; in the course of their stay they might start divorce proceedings, find out about getting an injunction, or discuss what they should do about their marital problems. However, for most battered women the stay allowed is too short to be helpful, and the stigma attached to referral to a psychiatric hospital is too great for this to be an acceptable solution, even in the short term.

Thirdly, help was likely to be withheld from women living with their husbands, but would be granted to the same women when living separately. The women themselves did not comment on this, but putting their accounts together it became clear that help, and particularly social work support, was much more readily available for women living as one-parent families than for women living with their husbands. There were two sides to this. Firstly, some husbands positively prevented their wives from receiving help, by forbidding their wives to receive 'the welfare' into the house, or by refusing help when it was offered. As Suzy said:

> 'I was offered home help because I was a bit ill after
> the baby was born and the health visitor said I
> needed help for a little while. My husband was away
> – he was in London. She got me the home help; he
> came home; and he says, "No, you're not; you do

your own housework." And he wouldn't let me have it. The doctor wanted to put me on tranquillisers but I still had to get up and look after the kids and do the housework.'

Q. *'So would you say the health visitor was helpful?'*
A. 'Yes, she tried to be. But everything she said, he said "no".'

Lisa, whose husband kept a café, was one of the women who was not allowed to have friends and whose attempts to get help had to be clandestine. She said:

'Three days after we were married, he said, "If you want to leave, don't ever think about it. Because I'll kill you before you leave me." I wanted to leave my husband a long time ago, but I'd got nowhere to go . . . I couldn't tell the health visitor my problems because he would just sit there and listen. I'd got to say, "Yeah, I'm all right, children's fine, yeah, yeah." Then I went to my doctor and I said, "I can't speak with the health visitor." So I arranged to meet her somewhere else. And she said, "Soon you've got to get out of that house. Sooner the better. You've got to leave him", she said. Then some other person took my health visitor's place and she started coming to the café as a customer because my husband didn't know her. Then we started talking. Of course, any time he comes along we've got to stop. But she made a report.'

Secondly it seemed to be assumed, particularly by social workers, that women bringing up children on their own were more in need of, and more deserving of, help than women living with their husbands. This idea is, of course, built into the social security system, which assumes that any woman living with a man as his wife will be financially supported by him. However, it also seems to apply in other areas. For example, several women, who were living with their husbands, would have appreciated day nursery places for their younger children, and the fact that such care was not available added to the difficulties of their lives: day nursery places went almost entirely to women bringing up children on their own.

The needs of single-parent families are of course, great;

however, it sometimes seems to be assumed that if a woman has a husband she has no need of any other help from statutory agencies. It is as though her needs are subsumed either under the heading of the welfare of the children, or under the heading of the welfare of the family. The 'invisibility' of the married woman has long antecedents: in 1910 for example, the report of the actuaries in relation to the proposed scheme of insurance against sickness stated, 'married women living with their husbands need not be included [in the insurance scheme] since where the unit is the family, it is the husband's and not the wife's health which it is important to insure' (Report of the Actuaries, 1910). It took many years and much hard work before it was fully acknowledged that the health care needs of married women could not be subsumed under the heading of 'husband' or 'family'. Similarly, today, married women have needs which are quite separate from those of their husband, of their children, or of the family as a whole. This point may seem trite; however, it lies behind much of the pressure exerted upon battered women to remain in their homes, as Maynard has shown (Maynard, this volume). For years before going to the refuge many of the women had desperately needed detailed advice about the possible courses of action which they might take, and support in making the decisions on behalf of themselves and their children. It seemed that so long as a woman remained within the home and the marriage there was a respect for the domestic authority of the husband which made it almost impossible for his wife to receive help if he did not wish that help to be given to her (McIntosh, 1978).

Fourthly, it seemed as if the views and the needs of the women themselves were often ignored or neglected. Partly this may be a consequence of the fact that abused women are often confused about what course of action is best for them and their children. Faced with the possibility of losing both home and marriage, both financial and social support, this confusion is hardly surprising. However, it does mean that those to whom they go for help must take account of what the women themselves see as appropriate help. Women may be looking for a different sort of help at an early stage in the marriage by comparison with a later stage, when violence has gone on for a longer time and attempts at reconciliation have proved fruitless (Dobash, Dobash and Cavanagh, this volume).

Lack of interest in the needs of women is in marked contrast to the energetic responsiveness of agencies when the welfare of children is thought to be threatened. Again, none of the women complained about this, but analysis of the interview material showed that a common theme was the use of children as a rationale for advice given to women. Some women might be advised to stay for the sake of the children and others to leave for the sake of the children; in either case the implication that the needs of the children should always come first was taken for granted both by the women themselves and by the people who abused them. In reality, it was the battered *mother* rather than the battered *woman* who was to be helped. (See also Parker, and Maynard, this volume, for further discussion of this point.)

Part I of this book has been concerned with one particular group of women, with the difficulties they faced, the help they sought and the decisions they made about their lives over a period of about two years. The story has been complicated because the women faced decisions which affected every aspect of their own and their children's lives. The aim has been to give the reader some insight both into the difficulties faced by abused women and into the ways they thought about the solutions which they themselves hoped to find. In Part II we turn to the broader context, and look at the legislative, social and economic framework within which these, and thousands of similar women, make their decisions.

PART II

Helping the abused woman and her children

Jan Pahl

I see no reason why every profligate fellow shall have the liberty to disturb a whole neighbourhood, and abuse a poor honest creature at a most inhuman rate, and is not to be called to account because it is his wife; this sort of barbarity was never so notorious and so much encouraged as at present, for every vagabond thinks he may cripple his wife at pleasure, and 'tis enough to pierce a heart of stone to see how barbarously some poor creatures are beaten and abused by merciless dogs of husbands.

It gives an ill example to the growing generation, and this evil will gain ground on us if not prevented. It may be answered, the law has already provided redress, and a woman abused may swear the peace against her husband, but what woman cares to do that? It is revenging herself on herself, and not without considerable charge and trouble.

How hard is it for a poor industrious woman to be up early and late, to sit in a cold shop, stall or market, all weathers, to carry heavy loads from one end of the town to the other, or to work from morning to night, and even then dread going home for fear of being murdered?
(Defoe, 1728)

Chapter seven

The legal background

Stephen Parker

Introduction

This chapter attempts to explain the legal structure within which battered women, and their advisers, must operate. In the space available, it is impossible to deal fully with every aspect of the law's application to domestic violence problems. In many cases, the legal provisions are extremely complex and they cut across the traditional boundaries that lawyers are trained to accept as natural (such as 'family law', 'property law', 'housing law', etc.). It is hoped that the account which follows is sufficient for a non-lawyer who comes into contact with the legal process and who wishes to understand procedures and terminology. In addition, practising lawyers who were trained before many of these remedies were introduced might find it useful to see how the provisions fit together (or don't, as the case may be) into a loose framework.

Three related themes underpin a critical approach to the law and battered women. The first is the ideology of privacy. Modern family law in England and Wales derives from a series of bourgeois legal changes in the mid- to late-nineteenth century. As such it is informed by a notion that the home is a private place, a haven in a heartless world, which is free from outside intervention. More cynically, it is a place where patriarchal power can be exercised without external restraints. The modern equivalent of this theory is a view that family law is 'pathological' (Eekelaar, 1971, p. 7); it only steps in when 'things go wrong'. As a result, divorce can only be obtained when the couple are living in separate households, family property rules are only applied on separation and the obligation to maintain is only properly enforceable when the parties are living apart. This facilitates 'hidden poverty' within the family if the income-receiver does not equitably distribute family resources (Pahl, 1980; Kidd, 1982).

On the face of it, domestic violence law departs from this non-interventionist approach. It permits orders to be made where the woman is not seeking a divorce, maintenance or custody. In the case of a non-molestation order, it may seek to control behaviour within the family unit; in other words, even where the couple have not separated. This leads into the second theme of the chapter. There is a vast gap between the law on the books and the law in action. Whereas on paper legal changes in the 1970s might be seen as progressive, in practice the judiciary has voluntarily cut down its own powers to use the law. And even where the Law Reports reveal judicial willingness to implement the powers available, one should note that generally only Court of Appeal cases are reported in this area. This means that the facts of these reported cases may have been exceptional (in so far as there is a norm to be departed from) and in the first instance judges in the lower courts might be unaware of, or might simply ignore, pronouncements from on high. Although this chapter is mainly concerned with explaining the law on the books, later chapters deal more fully with its application in practice.

The third theme which may emerge from this account is the complexity and lack of integration of legal remedies. It is scandalous that a body of rules intended to give protection against physical and mental abuse should be unintelligible to most of its users. It is probable that the present political climate is hostile to legal changes which might benefit women, nevertheless there is in existence a Law Commission (which includes a leading family lawyer) whose task is to codify the law. It has been silent on these matters (although it has recently recommended changes which would give banks and other mortgagees priority over a wife's interest in the matrimonial home (Law Commission, 1982).

In the interests of clarity, the following exposition of the law looks at various actions separately, although in practice they may be related or overlap. The discussion is centred on the problems of battered wives and the remedies available to cohabitees are stated separately.

The law

1 Divorce
It is frequently overlooked that divorce may be the principal legal response to domestic violence, rather than Domestic Violence Act injunctions or magistrates' orders. In theory, there is only one ground for divorce; that the marriage has broken down irretrievably. However, 'irretrievable breakdown' can only be proved by establishing one of five 'facts'. These can be summarized as (a) adultery; (b) unreasonable behaviour; (c) desertion for two years; (d) separation for two years where the other party consents to the divorce; and (e) separation for five years where there need not be consent.

In 1980, over 150,000 divorce decrees were granted and 70 per cent of the petitioners were women. The most 'popular' fact used was (b), unreasonable behaviour. This accounted for 33 per cent of all divorces and women comprised 89 per cent of the petitioners under it. Not surprisingly, the courts have failed to establish any clear test as to what behaviour is unreasonable. It seems clear in practice, however, that the majority of petitions under fact (b) include allegations of violence and they usually succeed if some of the violent incidents can be corroborated and at least one of them was within six months of the couple's separation.

Of course, these statistics may hide the true level of domestic violence underlying many divorces. A petitioner may rely on two or five year's separation (if that is possible) and it might be the violent husband who actually presents the petition. If a separation fact can be used then it is probably preferable to alleging unreasonable behaviour. Corroborative evidence is usually easier to come by and it avoids the distress of recollecting past experiences. On the other hand, a battered wife might use fact (b) rather than a separation fact if the violence is so severe as to be regarded by the divorce court as 'gross and obvious' misconduct (*Watchel* v. *Watchel* [1973] 1 All ER 829). She might then receive a larger property or maintenance order than she would otherwise have had (assuming that she wants it and there are sufficient resources anyway).

There is a point in stressing divorce as a remedy for domestic violence. The divorce itself should not involve a court appearance – although the custodial parent must attend a short interview to discuss the arrangements for the children – and solicitors ought to know what they are doing. Financial matters can be dealt with as part of the process and the court can transfer the home to the woman, whether it is freehold, a private tenancy or a council property.

If the woman is in fear of violence during the divorce process itself or wishes to exclude the husband from the home, this can be achieved by applying for an 'interlocutory injunction'. An interlocutory injunction simply means one granted during the course of other proceedings; in our case a divorce or judicial separation. The injunction might be a 'non-molestation order' or might go further and exclude the husband from the home. Technically, once the divorce proceedings and ancillary matters such as custody and property are over, the court loses jurisdiction to grant an injunction under this heading (because it is no longer inter-locutory). Nevertheless, it appears that the rules are bent where children's interests are directly affected (*Stewart* v. *Stewart* [1973] 1 All ER 313; *Beard* v. *Beard* [1981] 1 All ER 783).

The divorce court decides whether to grant non-molestation orders, exclusion orders and powers of arrest (which can be attached to either) on the same principles as are applied under the Domestic Violence Act 1976, and we discuss them more fully below.

2 The Domestic Violence and Matrimonial Proceedings Act 1976
Before this Act came into force, a woman could only obtain an injunction if she sought a divorce or judicial separation. In other words, the courts insisted that *all* injunctions had to be interlocutory. This is the earliest example of judges voluntarily cutting down their own powers. One suspects that the ideology of family privacy motivated this policy because, as one judge admitted, there was no legal authority making them do so (Ormrod J. in *Montgomery* v. *Montgomery* [1964] 2 All ER 22 at 238).

When the problem of battered women (or violent men) resurfaced in the 1970s it was felt that this practice either deterred women from seeking injunctions (because they were not prepared for divorce) or pushed them into a divorce which they were not ready for (Parker, 1981, 85). Partly as a result of this, the Domestic Violence Act 1976 ('the DVA') was passed. This permitted any county court to make orders (a) restraining the respondent from molesting the applicant or a child living with the applicant; (b) excluding him from the home or a specified area in which the home is included; or (c) ordering the respondent to allow the applicant back into the home (DVA, s.1(1)). Any or all of these orders can be made without the need for other proceedings, such as divorce, to be taken.

Section 2 of the Act included a novel provision. It allowed the judge to attach a power of arrest to any of the above orders if he (sic) is satisfied that the respondent has caused actual bodily harm to the applicant or child concerned and considers he is likely to do so again. The effect of a power of arrest is that it enables a constable to arrest without warrant a person whom he (sic) has reasonable cause of suspecting of being in breach of the non-molestation or exclusion order by reason of the suspect's use of violence or, as the case may be, of his entry into any premises. Once a person has been arrested under the power he must be brought before a judge within twenty-four hours and he must not be released within that period except on the direction of that judge. In reckoning the twenty-four hour period, no account is taken of any Sunday, Christmas Day or Good Friday.

Those, then, are the basic provisions of the Act as they affect married people. We can now look at their significance and the way the courts have restricted the value of them. The basic orders which can be granted are straightforward. Although the Act does not say so, the Court of Appeal has decided that a non-molestation order can only be granted where there is evidence of actual molestation (*Spindlow* v. *Spindlow* [1979] 1 All ER 169). Molestation, however, is a wider term than actual violence. It includes threats of violence and pestering, or as one judge put it recently, 'any conduct which can properly be regarded as such a degree of harassment as to call for the intervention of the court' (Ormrod L.J. in *Horner* v. *Horner* [1982] 2 All ER 495 at 497g).

101

Whilst this reasoning might seem circular – because we want to know *what* degree of harassment calls for the courts' intervention – the reported cases do not indicate that a restrictive interpretation of 'molestation' is being taken.

The Act does not lay down guidelines or criteria on which exclusion orders are to be based. Unlike the magistrates' powers (discussed below) violence is *not* a pre-requisite (*Spindlow*, above and Lord Scarman in *Davis* v. *Johnson* [1978] 1 All ER 1132 at 1156c). Nevertheless, there is disturbing evidence that the effectiveness of exclusion orders (whatever it might be) is being undermined in three respects. Firstly, guidance has been given to county court judges suggesting that time limits should be attached to exclusion orders. A Practice Note ([1978] 2 All ER 1056) states that, 'In most cases a period of up to three months is likely to suffice in the first instance.' As a result, unless the woman is prepared to keep coming back to court and asking for an extension, accommodation problems must still be sorted out, either by seeking a divorce or finding somewhere else to live. As we will see, the problem is particularly acute for battered cohabitees because they cannot use the divorce court.

The second inroad into exclusion orders results from a widening split within the judiciary as to what evidence is required before a man is to be excluded. The reported cases indicate two distinct approaches. The first concentrates on providing accommodation for the children. This line of reasoning, promoted by Lord Justice Ormrod (who has now retired), argues that investigations into the man's conduct should be minimised. Instead, the court should look to the question of who will be keeping the children and then exclude the other adult. The Law Reports indicate this to be the dominant approach (see, for example, *Spindlow*, above; *Walker* v. *Walker* [1978] 3 All ER 141; *Samson* v. *Samson* [1982] 1 All ER 780).

One might object to this approach, in that it is designed to protect the battered *mother* rather than the battered woman, but it may be thought preferable to an alternative line of cases which is emerging. Here, a more detailed enquiry is made into the man's conduct and its gravity is weighed against the consequences to him of being excluded from the home (see, for example, *Elsworth* v. *Elsworth* (1979) 9 Fam. Law 21; *Myers* v. *Myers* [1982] 1 All ER 776). The disturbing aspect of this trend is that the victim becomes an onlooker in an argument over whether the man's conduct warrants the likely consequences *to him* of being ousted from the home.

From a strictly legal point of view, the 'children approach' of Lord Justice Ormrod is more authoritative. However, one simply does not know the extent to which judges at county court level follow one line or the other. This leads us to the third worrying feature of the courts' policy on exclusion orders, namely, a widely alleged reluctance to make them *whatever the test*. There has been no substantial survey of the operation of the DVA, however the evidence collected by the Women's Aid Federation indicates that under 50 per cent of women who apply for exclusion orders are successful (Binney, Harkell and Nixon, 1981, 85).

This tendency of the judiciary to cut down its own powers is also evident if we look further at powers of arrest. These powers are almost unique in English (and Welsh) law because they bring the police into questions of enforcing civil orders. Without a power of arrest, the woman must take enforcement proceedings herself and these can be slow and traumatic. Further, the man might feel there is little to deter him from breaching the order where no power of arrest has been attached, (Binney, Harkell and Nixon, 1981, 85).

Despite the obvious advantages to a woman in having this power to call the police with some hope that they might actually turn up, there are a number of obstacles. In the first place, the DVA itself imposes restrictions. Looking again at section 2 we can see that actual bodily harm must already have been caused before the power can be attached. This led to an absurd result in one case where the husband actually threatened the wife from the witness box in court. The trial judge attached a power of arrest to the order but it was removed on appeal because the judge had not heard any evidence that actual bodily harm had been caused (*McClaren* v. *McClaren* (1979) 9 Fam. Law 153).

Difficulties over the wording of the section have been amplified by judicial practice. The Court of Appeal has decided that powers of arrest are exceptional remedies. In

Lewis v. Lewis [1978] 1 All ER 729 (at 731d) Ormrod J. said, 'a power of arrest is not to be regarded as a routine remedy by any means; quite plainly from the wording of s.2(1) it is an exceptional circumstance.' It is true that the requirement of actual bodily harm is a restriction not imposed elsewhere in the Act – so in that sense it is exceptional – but actual bodily harm is quite routine in these cases. The courts seem to have confined the statute. The statistics for 1980 confirm this. Out of 6,400 injunctions granted under s.1 of the DVA, only 24 per cent had powers of arrest attached to them. The regional variations are also startling. In the north-east, the figure was only 10 per cent, thus confirming the point made earlier that county court judges can act relatively autonomously from the law on paper.

The limitations on attaching powers of arrest have now been institutionalised by Practice Note [1981] 1 All ER 224. As a result of the alleged burden imposed on the police by the need to retain indefinitely orders containing a power of arrest, judges are now told that powers of arrest should normally not last for more than three months in the first instance. This parallels the three-month restriction on exclusion orders. As far as is known, the Lord Chancellor's Office undertook no empirical work to determine whether powers of arrest are invoked after three months. In any event, the mere presence of such a power might be what stops the man from breaching the order. The measure seems designed solely for the convenience of the police. Whilst a centralised data-bank, which has been called for (Freeman, 1979, 211), may not be realistic in the present climate, a filing cabinet is not an unknown information retrieval system.

In conclusion, the Domestic Violence Act promised to provide necessary (although not sufficient) protection for battered women. Its subsequent interpretation and application, however, are leading to general disillusionment with the civil law's ability to give that protection.

3 The Matrimonial Homes Act 1967

This Act was passed in order to strengthen and codify a spouse's occupation rights in the matrimonial home. The county court is empowered to make an order, *inter alia*, prohibiting, suspending or restricting the exercise by either spouse of the right to occupy (MHA 1967, s.1(2) as amended by DVA 1976, s.3). Although not particularly intended to deal with marital violence, the Act could be used in place of an exclusion order under the Domestic Violence Act and the Court of Appeal has accepted that the two jurisdictions are identical (*Harding* v. *Harding* (1980) 10 Fam. Law 146). Unlike the DVA, criteria for deciding whether to make such an order are laid down. A judge must have regard to the conduct of the spouses in relation to each other, to their respective needs and financial resources, to the needs of the children and to all the circumstances of the case (MHA 1967, s.1(3)).

A possible advantage in using this Act is that, in theory, the Practice Note restricting exclusion orders to three months' duration does not apply; although a judge would still be free so to limit an order under the 1967 Act.

The more important reason for mentioning the Matrimonial Homes Act 1967 is to strengthen the point made earlier that the law is confusing and lacks integration: and no one seems to be doing anything about it. One wonders how even the most conscientious solicitor can make imaginative and constructive use of legal remedies if s/he is only hanging on by the fingertips as to what these remedies are. This argument is compounded if we look at the parallel jurisdiction of the magistrates' courts.

The Domestic Proceedings and Magistrates' Courts Act 1978

The magistrates' court was first given a matrimonial jurisdiction in 1878, in response to a wave of public concern over wife beating. Exactly a century later, and during a similar period of concern, the jurisdiction was re-vamped. We deal here only with domestic violence remedies, but it should be noted that the magistrates' court also has powers to order periodical payments, a lump sum of up to £500 (the present limit) and legal custody or access.

The domestic violence remedies in the 1978 Act are very similar to those in the DVA. A 'personal protection order', which is the equivalent of a non-molestation injunction in the county court, can be granted. An exclusion order can also be made and a power of arrest can be attached to either. Despite the obvious similarities between these orders and those available under the DVA, there are annoying differences which, from a lawyer's point of view, generally make the magistrates' court a less desirable form.

Firstly, the personal protection order can only be made if the respondent has used, or threatened to use, violence against the applicant or a child of the family (DPMCA 1978, s.16(2)). As a consequence, the order only restrains violence or violent threats and a husband who 'merely' harasses the wife will not be in breach of the order (*Horner* v. *Horner* [1982] 2 All ER 495). A county court molestation order is therefore the more appropriate legal response to a male who pesters rather than assaults because it is not tied to violence.

Secondly, exclusion orders can only be made if certain conditions are met, whereas in the county court there is a general discretion. These conditions are complicated. Put simply, the respondent must actually have been violent to someone or be in breach of a personal protection order. Furthermore, the applicant (or child) must be in danger of being physically injured by the respondent (s.16(3)). This danger need not be imminent, but is judged objectively rather than from the applicant's point of view (*McCartney* v. *McCartney* [1981] 1 All ER 597). There is no scope, therefore, for the child-centred approach of some county courts whereby a male might be excluded without any violence being proved. A final point on exclusion orders in the magistrates' courts is that they cannot exclude the male from a specified area in which the home is included. In the county court, the DVA permits this, and many orders do prescribe a radius within which the respondent may not enter.

Thirdly, the power of arrest differs slightly in the magistrates' court (DPMCA. s.18). Although the conditions for attaching the power are very similar, the consequences of breach might not be. Under the 1978 Act, the arresting constable must bring the respondent before a magistrate within twenty-four hours. Unlike the DVA, however, there is no requirement to keep the man in custody until the appearance. If no power of arrest is attached to the order, the woman herself must take enforcement proceedings in respect of any breach. To do this, she must apply to a local magistrate for a warrant for the husband's arrest.

Despite the limitations mentioned above, the magistrates' court ought to be the preferred remedy for many domestic violence cases. It is cheaper than the county court, probably nearer, less formal and can grant orders such as maintenance and custody. The small amount of research conducted into the 1978 Act, however, indicates that the magistrates' courts are not popular with solicitors (Welsh Women's Aid, 1980a; McCann, 1981). One dominant criticism is that magistrates require more evidence of violence than do county court judges. This might be explained by magistrates' preoccupation with criminal cases where the standard of proof is higher than in civil ones.

Cohabitees

Of the remedies described above for married women, only interlocutory injunctions and Domestic Violence Act orders are available to cohabitees. The DVA remedies are expressly applied to 'a man and a woman who are living with each other in the same household as husband and wife' (DVA 1976, s.1(2) and 2(2)). There is now a handful of guides on cohabitation law (see Rights of Women, 1981, for a clear and committed exposition for non-lawyers; Parry, 1981, for a social worker's guide; Parker, 1981, for a more turgid legal analysis).

After a bizarre beginning, when it was doubted whether the Act could be used to exclude a property-owning cohabitee, it seems that the courts are now willing to apply the Act fully (*Davis v. Johnson* [1978] 1 All ER 1132). Although cohabitees are defined as those who *are* living with each other, the cases indicate that the courts will still assume jurisdiction if molestation occurs within a reasonable time of separation (*McLean v. Nugent* (1979) 123 Solic. Jo. 521). Furthermore, it is unlikely that enquiries will be made into the extent to which their relationship resembled that of husband and wife (*Adeoso v. Adeoso* [1981] 1 All ER 109).

If the DVA cannot be used, perhaps because there was too long a gap between separation and molestation, an interlocutory injunction could be sought. Obviously, this could not be ancillary to divorce proceedings, because they are not married to each other; however it could be pegged on to a nominal claim for damages in assault, trespass or nuisance (Parker, 1981, Chapter 7).

The main problem for a battered cohabitee concerns accommodation. In the absence of any court powers to transfer property rights on a permanent basis, any exclusion order will be only temporary protection where the man has a property interest because of the three-month time limit. Matters have been made worse by the Housing Act 1980. In the course of giving public sector tenants security of tenure, this Act deprived local authorities of the power to remove a violent man from the rent book and vest the tenancy exclusively in the woman.

Conclusion

The purpose of this chapter has been to provide an outline of the remedies which battered women can seek in the civil courts. As with most renditions of the law, there is an air of unreality about it. There is now a widespread feeling that injunctions do not deter violent males, particularly where no power of arrest has been attached, and that the small protection offered is not worth the trauma. It is quite possible that the most important legal instrument for battered women is the Housing (Homeless Persons) Act 1977 which placed local authority housing responsibilities on a statutory footing (Binney, Harkell and Nixon, this volume). Because the Act is discussed fully in chapter 11 it is not elaborated here.

Those readers who have struggled through to the end of this chapter may now feel that the introductory remarks were justified. Judges have failed to use fully the powers given to them and the legal rules are hopelessly complicated and intertwined. Throughout, there is a feeling of reluctance to intervene in the family unit until something final, such as a divorce, is being pursued. Thus the law reflects and helps reproduce the ideology of privacy which is central to the problem in the first place.

One is not hopeful about possible legal changes. In the short term, divorce could be made easier (or on demand) and this might defuse some conflict. Conciliation procedures could be extended to remove disputes from a court setting. The law on injunctions could be simplified and rationalised. But all these have their problems. To change divorce laws at the moment invites reactionary pressure to cut down women's property rights, justified on the vague basis that 'the pendulum has swung too far'. Conciliation procedures can turn into reconciliation procedures where women are pressed to give the relationship another chance. And no amount of codification will stop judges at ground level from subverting the legal protections that exist on paper.

In the long term, law has even less to offer. By individualising disputes, law deflects attention away from the *social* nature of problems. If it is true that domestic violence can only be understood in the context of economic and social subordination of women, then legal change can have only marginal effect. A thorough exorcism of the sexist ideology which pervades the law would remove one prop of a patriarchal order (Freeman, 1980) but the structure would hardly topple. The struggle is political.

Chapter eight

The police response to violence against women in the home

Tony Faragher

How effective are the police in helping women who have been assaulted within the home? Are the police likely to be effective in preventing further violence? How do the police view their own role in this area of work? If there is agreement that changes in police practice are necessary, what realistically are the chances of these being brought about? This chapter will attempt to answer these questions and will consider the role of the police in helping abused women.

Legal statute, in theory, provides adequate redress and protection for women who are assaulted by men within the home, within marriage or a marriage-like relationship. One group of legal practitioners, the police, have on occasions stated that the law is adequate as it stands:

> The Offences Against the Person Act 1861, which in the main covers the whole field of this subject, has been in operation for many years now and the penalties and powers under that and other Acts appear amply adequate. (Select Committee on Violence in Marriage, 1975, p. 377)

The powers and duties laid down under this Act of 1861, which among other things specifies technical definitions of various severities of assault ranging from common assault through to grievous bodily harm with intent, have recently been augmented by two pieces of legislation. The Domestic Violence and Matrimonial Proceedings Act 1976 and the Magistrates' Courts Act 1978 have given to the police and the wider legal system the authority and the means to intervene decisively where women have been assaulted by men. Yet still in practice there is a yawning gap between abstract rights and actual remedies, a gap that has been narrowed but little by the recent decade of public debate and legislative reform. The arguments that will be advanced in the following pages are based in large part on empirical research carried out in 1978-9, a time when at least some of the above mentioned legal reforms had been implemented. While one might wish to make specific criticisms of the police with a view to improving the service available to women who have been assaulted in marriage, these criticisms need to be viewed in perspective, for the police are but one element in a legal system that as a whole consigns the problem of marital violence to a status of relative unimportance. The police are undoubtedly the most visible and accountable part of the legal system, but to focus criticism narrowly and exclusively on them is to run the risk, highlighted by Gouldner, of scapegoating the 'bureaucratic caretakers' while at the same time obscuring and neglecting critical analysis of the 'master [sic] institutions' (Gouldner, 1975). While it must be left to others to advance the broad theme of the relationship between the structures of male dominance and the structures of the state (Hanmer, 1978), let it suffice to say that the police are clearly not an anachronistic part of the social structure perpetuating what have elsewhere become redundant social values. The police, and in turn the rest of the legal system itself, operate so as to leave essentially untouched the power relationships within the family. In short, the dominance of men over women is enhanced by legal non-intervention, as is the legitimacy of male violence.

The police have the potential for being an important agency in any pattern of services for battered women. They may act as a 'gateway', a point of access and a signpost to other sources of assistance. As the sole agency that is available twenty-four hours a day on a comprehensive, geographical basis, one would expect them to be a first and major contact for many battered women. Such expectations are, however, contra-dicted by the facts. Dobash and Dobash (1980, 164) showed that, in their sample of women, only 2 per cent of violent incidents had been reported to the police. Another recent study indicates that 61 per cent of women passing through refuges had at some stage contacted the police (Binney et al., 1981, 14). Although the majority of battered women will at some stage in their help-seeking 'career' have contacted the police, they will have sought help from the police after only a minority of violent episodes. Although most frequently contacted, two studies reveal that the police were rated lowest of all agencies in terms of being helpful. Binney et al. (1981) report a figure of 64 per cent of women nationally who classed their contact with the police as 'unhelpful', while the corresponding figure in Pahl's more localised study was 71 per cent (Pahl, this volume). As Sainsbury has demonstrated in the context of the personal social services, those who seek help are most likely to rate services highly, and persist in seeking further help, if, and only if, the services offered are congruent with their initial conceptions of what it is they need. The response of the police, based, as will be argued, on notions of mediation and restoration of the peace, falls far short of women's initial and unschooled expectations of protection and legal redress (Sainsbury, 1975).

What then is the response of the police to cases of marital violence? In 1978 I was grateful to be granted permission to observe the work of the Staffordshire Police Force. Working from the communications room of two urban police stations it was possible to rendezvous with the motorised police patrols ('incident response vehicles') at the scene of twenty-six 'domestic disputes' and to observe the methods by which the police dealt with them.

The methodological problems and implications of this observational research are dealt with more fully elsewhere (Faragher, 1980). The following conclusions can be drawn from the observational data. By no means all of the incidents to which the police were called, and which the researcher observed, were cases in which assault had taken place. The researcher took care to validate independently whether injury had been caused or not. Indeed many of the incidents to which the police were called could be termed 'domestic disputes' with complete accuracy. This fact, and the concomitant expectation that all such cases are likely to be trivial (even if important to the parties involved), is the context in which police officers tackle their next call to a 'domestic'.

The numerical breakdown for the twenty-six observed cases

is as follows. Ten out of twenty-six (38 per cent) contained an infringement of the legal code which, had the police so wished, could have formed the basis for a charge and subsequent arrest. In more detail, five of these ten cases involved assault, two involved breaches of injunctions and the remaining three cases involved damage and/or theft by ex-husbands or ex-boyfriends.

With regard to the five assault cases all would, under the terms laid down in the Offences Against the Person Act 1861, be properly classified as Section 47 offences – assault occasioning actual bodily harm. In two out of these cases an arrest was made, although in one of the two it was clear that the arrest was made primarily because of the presence of an observer. Had the researcher not been present it is certain that the husband would have managed to persuade the officers not to arrest. The following case study (quoting directly from the researcher's field notebook written up after attending each incident) illustrates how police officers did not carry out an arrest, even though the mandate for doing so was clearly laid down in a standing instruction issued by their own police force:

Injured party had two black eyes, of which one was badly watering. She had been severely beaten around the face, with bruising also on the bridge of the nose. Her lip and mouth were cut, bruised and swollen. Her hands were also cut. On arrival the WPC took close look at eye and asked whether husband had done it. She replied in the affirmative. WPC also asked if she had anywhere to go – she replied she had not. Woman said she wanted to get back into her house as it was *hers*, she had paid for it even though it was in his name. WPC replied that if that was the case then the position in law was that it was his house. She was also asked if she wanted to make a complaint about the assault. She replied that she did as she did not want him to get away with it this time. They asked again if she wanted to make a statement and she said yes. They drove her to her house two streets away. Husband came to the door and appeared to be expecting the police. He was calm and offered no resistance to the patrol entering: he welcomed them in. At this point the woman explained what had happened – her husband had accused her of going with other men and had called her a whore, etc. Once she started to explain this the couple started to argue. Both officer (PC and WPC) said this was not the kind of language to be used in front of the children. Older child took the baby to bed. Patrol asked the man what had happened and why the assault had taken place. He replied it was due to too much drink. She retorted that it was because she was being unfairly accused of being a slag. Patrol told her to shut up at one point because she was interfering. PC looked at her and used strong language to finally shut her up. WPC asked her to state categorically whether she was going to make a complaint. She again replied that she was.

PC said he wanted to have a word with her outside the room. Once the couple were in different rooms WPC started to talk to the man (I was in the room with them). She asked whether there was likely to be any repetition of the assault that night. He turned and said, 'I don't think so.' He repeated this twice, and she asked him to clarify. Eventually he said it was highly unlikely. He then spoke to the WPC at some length (2-3 mins.) about how difficult it was to talk to her when she was in drink. 'You can't take that kind of lip off a woman.' He stated that he did a lot around the house – decorating – and that several days ago he had painted a wall and she had come home and abused him about the colour. He said he didn't want to put up with it any more. WPC asked him if he could put a curb on her drinking – 'No.'

WPC told him that they would summons him if wife wanted but that they did not have the time to spend taking statements if the woman was going to retract. (At this point the woman re-entered the room.) WPC said to the woman that if she still wanted to make a complaint she should come into the police station the next day. Woman asked what protection did she have that night. What if there was a repetition? WPC replied that it was up to her to make sure there was not a repetition. The patrol left. Back at the police station I asked the PC what he had been talking to the woman about in the other room. He said she had been going on about how her husband kept raking up the past. PC said he had advised her to forget about it all and to start worrying about the children.

The rates of arrest from the observed cases are congruent with the experience of women passing through refuges nationally. In only 20 per cent of life-threatening cases was an arrest made. In cases where there was severe bruising or black eyes not resulting in hospital admission the arrest rate was 15 per cent (Binney *et al.*, 1981, p. 15).

There was clear evidence from the observed cases that the police were ineffective in enforcing the terms of injunctions, or of assisting women householders to enforce injunctions. One woman who asked the police to remove her separated husband from the house was informed, 'We don't evict people, that is a matter for the courts. We are only there to prevent a breach of the peace.' The woman had an injunction against her husband preventing him from entering the house, although it had not got a power of arrest attached. Although the Domestic Violence and Matrimonial Proceedings Act 1976 reformed existing law so as to make the relief obtained by injunctions independent of the substantive relief offered by divorce, the police felt unable to aid this particular woman because of her status as 'wife'. Even though she was not living with her husband and had an injunction against him, this status overrode both the presence of the injunction and the right of any citizen to call for the assistance of the police if someone refuses to leave their home. In the second case concerning an injunction there was a breakdown of administrative systems to the extent that the officers dealing with the case were unaware that an injunction was in force. Only a chance remark by a neighbour worried about the noise of arguing and fighting next door alerted the police to the fact that an injunction was in force. They had already visited the house earlier in the evening. The assaulted woman had not at that time informed the police about the injunction. Later (after her separated husband's eventual arrest) she disclosed that she had been too terrified to tell the police in front of her husband that she had an injunction. The injunction itself was seen by the police as being the private business of the woman; immediately prior to his arrest her husband was asking her if she was going to 'go against him'. The officers present did

115

nothing to emphasise that he had broken the terms of an order emanating from a court. Despite the fact that the woman had made public the dispute by enlisting the aid of external sources of authority (the police, the courts, the law), in the last analysis it was still perceived as being her private problem. Hers had to be the casting vote, so to speak, in the decision over whether an arrest was to be made.

Three observed cases involved theft and damage. In all three the damage had been caused by ex-husbands or ex-boyfriends and was clearly part of a campaign of harassment and retribution. In one case the damage was extensive, consisting of several smashed windows, a wrecked Christmas tree and presents, and a table and chairs destroyed. In another case a sofa was slashed with a knife, while in the third case the woman alleged that she and her second husband had been assaulted by her ex-husband, who then proceeded to load the contents of her home into a van. In all three cases the police declined to take legal action for damage or theft.

In summary, it is worth noting that violence had ceased in all cases by the time the police patrol arrived. Although the verbal disputes were sometimes extremely unpleasant, in none of the cases did the difficulties arise that the police often quote. For instance, there were no cases of women attacking police officers in defence of their husband, nor was it necessary to restrain any of the participants. Similarly there were no instances where it was difficult for the police to enter premises. Permission to enter was invariably given by the (male) householder.

It is important to comprehend the police understanding of why women fail to press charges, as the failure of women to do so is the reason most often cited by the police as to why their intervention serves little purpose. It is part of the common wisdom of the police station, reinforced through training school, that women will inevitably withdraw their complaints and will fail to co-operate in legal proceedings. A long-serving policeman sums up the frustrations and futility that the police believe to be an inescapable part of their dealing with battered women:

'you may get a thing develop this afternoon and you are stuck with the possibility, well, invariably when you have arrested a man and brought him to the station, within two or three hours the wife starts thinking, well, where is the money going to come from, who is going to support the kids and she is up here asking for him to be bailed out. So our dilemma is do we bail the man and let him go back to continual assault or do we shove him in front of the court in the morning and let the magistrate decide and then of course we will invariably ask for conditions for him not to go within three miles of the home, something like that, which is very often done and then the case is put through the normal way. It might take three months for it to come to court and in the interim period as it's happened with me, I've gone down to the house to see how everything is progressing and hubby is in bed. 'What is he doing here? The court order says he must not come within three miles'. 'Oh we've made it up' they tell us. You see, so you know when the thing is going to come to court – really it's flogging a dead horse. From the police view we've got no axe to grind, we couldn't care less, but it does seem a lot of public money being wasted in prosecution which when it gets to court she is all for having it scrubbed. . . .'

The degree of police concern over possible withdrawal of the complaint is not matched, however, by the frequency with which this occurs in practice. Only one in ten women in a local study were found to have withdrawn their complaint (Dawson and Faragher, 1977, 142). The only way in which this low level of withdrawal can be accounted for is that the police are extremely selective about who they sponsor to take legal action. This is borne out by observation at the scene of 'domestics' – women are time and again asked whether they *really* want to take legal action. Alternatively women are given time to 'think it over' in the belief that an 'unemotional' decision made the next day will be more realistic. In this sense the police abrogate their protective role, for their judgment is heavily influenced by prognoses of the woman's reliability as a witness in court proceedings.

Thus the police evaluate the need for their intervention by the degree to which the woman appears to be prepared to embark on legal action. An unwillingness to proceed may be

117

interpreted as capriciousness, or perhaps an indication that things cannot be serious. Little or no account is taken of other factors, perhaps most importantly the psycho-social effects of battering. In their proposals for a research strategy on violence to women in the home, Women's Aid Federation (England) see clear parallels between the effects of torture on prisoners and the effects of violence by men against women:

> The constant pressures of the violent situation are debilitating; the experience of fear, pain, confusion and humiliation leads to a paralysis which is not easily shed. Beyond the initial confusion, apathy or despair . . . we note a continuing loss of confidence, energies and initiative, an inability to cope with officialdom and authoritarian personalities, and difficulty in making decisions. (Women's Aid Federation (England) Research Group, 1981, p. 13)

This is the backdrop against which an almost immediate decision is required from the women. Having just been assaulted she will be asked, in all likelihood in the presence of her husband, whether she wishes to take legal action. The decision is a momentous one and carries with it the necessity to make simultaneous decisions about housing, income, and an unknown life. Failure to take the decision swiftly is, as has been noted above, likely to be taken as an indication that the problem is not sufficiently serious to warrant police interventions.

It is not only in the case of violence against women that the police need to be certain they have a complainant who will be prepared to take legal action. The need for a complainant marks out the public domain from the private, and distinguishes those areas of work that are conceived by the police as central from those that are considered marginal. A brief examination of the conditions under which the police demand a complainant helps make clear the context within which the police respond to violence against women within the home.

Police definitions of 'public' and 'private'

The dividing line between what the police see as 'private' and what as truly a matter for public concern is not well

118

understood outside police circles. The following three examples, taken from police records, show clearly that the police are reluctant to take legal action in a variety of situations unless the injured party (IP) wishes to do so.

(Case 600) 'At about 4.a.m. Wed. 3.2.78 I assaulted my brother-in-law John Smith. I put him in hospital. Mr Smith will not inform the police who assaulted him but I wish to confess I did it.'

(IP refused to make statement of complaint. IP visited in hospital.)

(Case 478) 'My son, Ian, 18 years, was beaten up on Thursday night at about 11.20 p.m. He was knocked unconscious and cannot recall the incident but still has swollen face and bruising.'

(IP did not want any action taken by the police for him. He still has slight bruising to the face.)

(Case 297) 'My boyfriend has been assaulted inside the XYZ Club tonight. He ran off and is somewhere in the town, possibly in hiding. He has a cut to his neck and ear. The guy who assaulted him is a Robert of Church Street.'

The researcher was present at the police station when the last of these cases (297) was reported. Although the complainant was adamant that something should be done, and although there was a prolonged discussion between her and the duty officer at the station enquiry desk, the police were firm in their insistence that there could be no arrest unless they received a complaint from the injured party. Moreover the police did not go out and search for the injured man, preferring him to contact them if he considered the matter sufficiently important.

On many occasions the police stated that the major part of their work consisted of events that were part of the private domain, that 'should not really have concerned us'. A large range of incidents are seen by the police as being extraneous to their real work. In the USA Wilson reports that dealing with domestic disputes is a much disliked task (J.Q. Wilson, 1968, 24), while in Britain Reiner reports his findings that domestic disputes and traffic control (especially school crossings) were seen as frustrating 'because of their apparent uselessness or extraneous character from the standpoint of a specific notion of real police work' (Reiner, 1978, 178).

Not only are 'domestics' thought by the police to lie in the private sphere, to be marginal to the tasks of 'real' police work and to offer little opportunity for the exercise of professional skill; the specific case of battered women raises contradictions and anxieties about the issue of popular support for the police:

> Policemen need to believe in a largely consensual populace whose values and standards they represent and enforce. It is by reference to this that they legitimate their activities. They are intermediaries who bring forth for punishment those whom 'most people' deem to deserve it. (Cain, 1973, 69).

More recently the same author has observed:

> Policemen themselves combine a paranoia about loss of public confidence (which has never been substantiated), with a contradictory belief that the 'mass of decent respectable people' are behind them. This endemic anxiety and contradiction means that highest status is accorded to work for which it is clear that there is popular support. Conversely, when there is a suspicion, based on previous life experience, or public political argument, that popular opinion is divided, ambivalent, or opposed, then the anxiety and concomitant reluctance to be involved is enhanced. (Cain, 1977, 158-9)

Given that there is cultural endorsement of violence as an appropriate means for the social control of women (Hanmer, 1978), intervention that would be seen by police and consensual public alike to discriminate positively in favour of battered women (because it ceased to discriminate *against* them) will be resisted by the police. The concern of the police may be to demonstrate that they are a caring and efficient organisation, while at the same time being seen as benign and accessible, without necessarily developing the kinds of skills that would enable them to deal constructively with the problems of battered women. In a pluralist society the notion of a consensual public – 'the community' – must necessarily remain an illusion. The police search for consent must in these circumstances take on the nature of a delicate balancing act, appeasing those who must be appeased, convincing all sections of society (or at least those sections of society that are defined by the police as constituting 'the community') that the kinds of policing on offer will meet their needs. Within this context the possibilities seem bleak for persuading and encouraging the police to develop more positive and more constructive services for battered women. The groups that represent battered women are in the last analysis seen by the police as neither unduly relevant to their search for consent, nor as sufficiently powerful to demand a response.

One has only to compare the response of the police (and the whole of the legal system) to 'mugging' with its response to 'battering' to understand that the promotion of measurable improvements of police response to battered women has been, and will continue to be, an arduous task. It is only with the greatest difficulty that the issue of violence against women can be placed on the police agenda, precisely because it is in every sense at the very margin of their work and role as they and society define it. Both phenomena – 'mugging' and 'battered women' – came to public notice at approximately the same time in the early 1970s. The idea of 'mugging' as a threat to cherished and central social values fell on fertile ground. Hall *et al.* (1978), in their extensive study of the social response to 'mugging', show how the police were eager to demonstrate the gravity, the dangers, and the fast growth of this new crime. The phenomenon of violence against women, though numerically infinitely more prevalent, met with remarkably different treatment. The records of the Select Committee show clearly that the importance of the phenomenon and the concomitant need for public intervention were vigorously contested. Within the social climate of the time, described as a 'coordinated swing towards tougher social discipline' (Hall *et al.*, 1978), the issue of mugging was without difficulty taken on board and the steps necessary to counter it promulgated vigorously by the police. The 'discovery' of violence against women in the home, on the other hand, threatened cherished values and laid bare the fact and method of the exercise of the power of men over women. Predictably it did not mobilise public resources.

Recent social events and significant shifts in police practice need to be mentioned briefly at this point. Perhaps in response to the street riots of the summer of 1981, perhaps in response more generally to the prevailing social climate, recent years have seen a growing distinction drawn between 'soft' policing, epitomised in the notion of 'community policing' in which the virtues are expounded of sensitivity to the needs of local communities and in which it is advocated there should be a broad coalition of interest between local police and community, and 'hard' policing with its accompanying structural differentiation into specialisms; riot control, anti-terrorism, armed patrols and so on. If violence against women was a peripheral element in 'real' police work in 1978 (the time at which the empirical material presented in this chapter was gathered), then it would seem more than probable that at the present time, within both models of policing, 'hard' and 'soft' domestic violence will be even more displaced from the centre of things. Violence against women is clearly not the concern of the 'hard' models of policing. Within the 'soft' model, with its accent on change by community consent, and the avoidance of the use of legal means of enforcement where possible, battered women will be unlikely to find any enhanced protection from violence or effective legal redress.

Proposals for change

Four main areas can be identified in which change is desirable and would improve the quality of police functions in relation to battered women: arrest, referral, training and the improvement of information systems. It is clear that there would need to be significant realignment of the police position as regards marital violence for any of these proposals for change to be implemented successfully. Firstly, there is arrest: it is proposed that an arrest should automatically be made whenever an assault has taken place, regardless of the wishes of the injured party. Only by this means can violence against women be converted to an issue automatically necessitating public intervention and women be guaranteed protection from further attack. The scope for discretionary decision making by individual officers would thus, in theory at least, be considerably lessened and postponed to a more appropriate stage of the legal process. The means to bring this about are, of course, considerably more problematic than the recommendation itself. Many police forces (including the one I studied) had issued written instructions precisely to the effect that arrest must be automatic. The scope for individual discretion, namely the power to redefine events so as to disguise the fact of assault, means that in practice such orders can effectively be countermanded. The internal problems of supervision of officers necessary to bring about this change are by no means insurmountable if the police service itself possesses the will to develop constructive services for battered women.

Secondly, it is essential that arrest should be accompanied by referral of the woman to a specialist agency such as Women's Aid who are able to provide the necessary services. It is recommended that referral should be to Women's Aid as they are the only national organisation that is geared to providing services for the group in question. As other chapters in this volume show, other agencies have neither the expertise nor resources (both practical and ideological) to act in a co-ordinating role for the whole range of services required by battered women. Individual women require services from widely scattered agencies in the crucial matters of housing, income and personal protection. It is important that a specialist agency is available to perform a sympathetic and informed signposting function, while at the same time providing personal support and protection. In making this recommendation it is recognised that Women's Aid does not at the present time have sufficient material resources to discharge this function adequately.

Thirdly, it would appear that there is relatively little emphasis placed on training for intervention in incidents of battering, because of the low status accorded to this area of work. Such training as does exist is focused on police techniques for mediation and restoration of the peace. In other words the focus is on public order rather than on relating to the needs of battered women. Similarly, training reflects the generalised assumption that all 'domestics' are by definition trivial unless proven otherwise. There is a need for training which will sensitise officers to the real problems of fear, pain, humiliation and a sense of helplessness, and which would equip them to make a more positive response. The expertise to carry out training of this sort is not necessarily to be found within the police service itself. It will surely be necessary for the police to reach outwards and buy in expertise, whether this takes the form of civilian personnel to run training programmes or whether it takes the form of preparation of training materials such as film and video of personal accounts of violence within the home.

Fourthly and finally, there is room for the improvement of information systems. Whereas the police nationally have embraced with vigour the new technology of information systems (witness the development of the Police National Computer which enables swift access to be made to the details of several million people and events), information storage and retrieval in what the police see as less important areas of their work is likely to be achieved by the older paperwork methods.

In the police force under study I witnessed several acute breakdowns of the information system where, for instance, officers were unaware of the existence of an injunction. Local knowledge within the police station of people and events can no longer be relied upon to provide officers with the appropriate information. There is a strong case for integrating information about violence in the home – incidents, sentences, individual histories and proclivities of violent men – into the modern computer system.

If, in response to this proposal, the objection is raised that it is an intrusion into a private sphere and an erosion of individual liberties, the counter question must be posed: 'Whose privacy? Whose liberty?'

Chapter nine

The response of social workers to domestic violence

Mary Maynard

Until recently our understanding of wife beating[1] has largely depended upon what battered women in refuges have had to say about their experiences. Although such work is very important it has always been recognised that women going to refuges represent only the 'tip of an iceberg'. For every woman who goes to a refuge many more in similar circumstances do not, for a variety of reasons. At least part of this 'invisibility' can be explained by the way in which 'family matters' are regarded in our society.

Numerous writers have remarked on the privatised nature of family life and on the fact that it is women who have borne the brunt of the privatisation process.[2] Woman, in the role of wife and mother, is regarded as being mainly responsible for the maintenance of the family unit. Her main task is to provide personal services for family members. Within this personal space, away from the public sphere, the private lives of those within the family are to be respected and supported. But in addition to providing protection from outside intrusion, the marriage relationship isolates a couple and their family from others. Thus any problems that occur within the relationship are viewed as private and individual troubles. The police called to a domestic dispute are expected to recognise the sanctity of marriage, embarrassed neighbours become socially distant and the woman who is battered guiltily tries to preserve her home at all costs.[3] In refusing to see the family as anything other than a haven of privacy, we turn a blind eye to the bruises and a deaf ear to those women who are experiencing the full force of their husband's aggression. For women who are beaten the very term *privacy* is an unfortunate misnomer for physical, social and emotional isolation.

However, despite this fabric of privacy the plight of battered women is not entirely hidden to some professions. Doctors see them, hospitals treat their injuries, marriage guidance counsellors console them and their distress is often displayed to other agencies of the welfare state. Key amongst these are social work departments. Social workers deal with a variety of 'social problems' and they inevitably come into contact with women who are beaten. To look at social work cases, then, is one means of gaining access to a number of battered women only some of whom may have been in contact with a refuge. However, an examination of the attitudes and practices involved in social workers' responses to domestic violence goes further than merely displaying the advice and help that may be made available. It also demonstrates how the routine and everyday activities of one welfare state agency are premised upon, and concerned to maintain, a particular image of familial relationships and of the status of wives in the family.

The study which forms the basis of this chapter is based on an analysis of current social work case files in one northern town.[4] It focuses on how social workers' practices are reported within such files. Case files are composed of diary-like entries written by social workers about each contact they have with their clients. They contain many repeated impressions of clients and their circumstances. Like jottings in a personal diary, the files describe the feelings social workers have about their clients and the nature of their problems as well as recording advice and action that has been offered. Periodically there is a case summary, providing a general impression of the case and how it is progressing. This is often a means of offering a short description of the client and the case to other social workers who might be involved. Case files, then, are records which are primarily kept to acquaint social workers with the details of a particular case. They are descriptions written strictly for consumption within the social work profession and would be seen by and sometimes have to be justified to, colleagues and superiors. Such files may not be an exact record of what happened in a particular instance and we can take it for granted that a certain amount of 'dressing up' goes on in the writing up of file material. Important from our point of view, however, is the audience for which the files are compiled – a professional group of social workers. During an interview, for example, respondents are likely to be pre-occupied with presenting a favourable image of themselves and their behaviour. By analysing the files we were able to look at how social workers presented and would try to justify themselves to themselves rather than how they would do this to the obtrusive and potentially threatening presence of the researcher.

The research discussed here was designed in such a way as to give a general picture of the social work department studied. Not all the case files were read. Instead a one in ten random sample of all current files was taken. This yielded a total of 103 for analysis.

The battered women[5]

The random selection of cases enables us to make generalisations about the number of battering cases routinely covered by social workers. Of the 103 social work case files that were analysed, thirty-four contained direct references to domestic violence. This was an unexpectedly high figure. During our initial liaison with the social work department we were warned about the danger of working with a relatively small sample size, not because it would be statistically unreliable but because the department expected that we would be lucky if we came across even one or two cases of wife beating. The thirty-four women we discovered indicate that the best estimate of the number of battering cases covered by the social work department in this average provincial town and its surrounding areas is 340. This represents 33 per cent of all current social work cases involving regular casework.

There are some difficulties in interpreting this figure. Firstly, not all instances of wife beating were recorded. Battering was not the central focus of most of the cases, as far as the social workers were concerned, and therefore the number of instances related in the files probably substantially underestimates the actual number of assaults. Secondly, the figures presented so far refer to ongoing social work cases which have at *some time* involved battering, rather than cases which indicate that violence is currently taking place. Concerned that this issue might undermine the overwhelming nature of our findings, we checked on how many women were being beaten during the two years immediately preceding our reading of the files. We found records indicating regular violence to six women within the previous two months. A further twenty-one women had been beaten during the preceding twelve months and six more women had been assaulted on occasions during the previous two years. It must be emphasised that these figures refer to those instances of beatings recorded by the social workers and not to the actual number of times a woman may have been battered. Finally, eight files provided only scanty information about the batterings, making it impossible to produce a detailed analysis. For the rest, however, there was substantial evidence of both repetitive and extensive violence frequently involving wounding and injury. For example one file reads: 'I was surprised to find she had a patch over her eye . . . and a lump and bruise on her forehead and a bruised hand.' And another: 'She said that . . . he had knocked her about. When he left, the place was in a terrible shambles and a policewoman had to clear the room up. He had smashed pots and pans and thrown a sauce bottle across the room.' A number of the assaults described on the case files involved the use of instruments. For instance:

'I was surprised to find that Dawn's head was heavily bandaged. She told me that this weekend her cohabitee . . . had brought out a humane killer and had reversed this and crashed it down on her skull.' [This woman attempts suicide.] 'She went on to describe beatings with shillelaghs, two of which hung on the wall as ornaments. She said that a middle-sized one no longer hung there as he (her husband) had recently broken it over her head, breaking her skin. She described severe punchings and 'kneeings', assaults with thrown objects (a plate of Ready Brek a week ago) and beatings in front of her friends.'

It is quite clear from these examples that social workers are well aware of the nature and extent of the violence that a significant proportion of their female clients are receiving. It is also apparent from the social workers' documentation that it is not only the physical injuries caused by the battering which are significant. The perpetual terror and foreboding of future attacks means that some women fear for their lives. In one case, 'This man's wife dialled 999 this evening in respect of her husband's aggressive threatening manner. She was afraid he would kill her.' Such fear is not unfounded but based upon actual threats made by the man which can be as psychologically harmful as the physical assaults themselves. To give just one example: 'He was threatening that he would make her suffer as he had suffered and spoke of killing her.'

This then confirms that the wife beating contained within our sample follows a similar pattern to that documented elsewhere. It involves real and serious physical assault, some of which is caused by the use of offensive weapons. Such violence is carried out in conjunction with threats and warnings, all of which mean that the women involved live in a permanent state of intimidation and fear. The evidence of the files seems to suggest that social workers are aware of all these aspects, at least in individual cases. Whether this indicates an awareness of the nature of battering in general is another question.

Advice and action offered by social workers

One of the first questions to be asked is, 'What do social workers do in terms of offering advice and action to wives who are beaten?' The straightforward answers can be itemised for our sample. Three couples were referred to the Marriage Guidance Council. Two women were immediately placed in a mental hospital after having been battered. One woman was advised to take a holiday. Several social workers had discussions on 'the problem' but this was usually with the woman only and rarely with the man *and* the woman, or the man on his own. Such talks seemed to have little obvious outcome. However, for the vast majority of women the files indicate that nothing was done to immediately relieve the situation. There are two references to social workers suggesting that the woman take out a separation order or start divorce proceedings but in seven instances where the women themselves begin to talk about separation or actually walk out of their homes the social workers dissuaded them. For example: 'She was thinking of leaving her husband again. Pointed out she had Christopher (son) to consider in this and her husband's feelings for the baby and herself. Reminded her that she had married and had to accept the consequences.' This last example indicates how children are used to encourage women to continue with marriages in which they are beaten.

The itemisation of the help given, however, does not sufficiently convey the remarkably unsympathetic ways in which social workers recorded their intervention. For example: (on visiting a woman and finding she has been beaten) 'I advised Mrs Blank not to argue with her husband too much and said that I would pop in to see her in a week or two.' Social workers were obviously loath to be seen to be agreeing with or siding with the women in their plight, particularly when the 'presenting problem' of the case (i.e. the one that they had initially been brought in to deal with) was related to others in the family. They continually emphasised their neutrality:

> 'I had again to explain my position to Mrs Blank. I said
> that I had to be seen to be neutral. I was there to help all
> members of the family. This I would be unable to do if
> the impression was given that I sided with any member
> of the family.'

The 'balanced view' approach to wife beating is part of general social worker attitudes and training. It is related to the idea that *professional* social workers do not get emotionally involved in the problems of their clients and is rooted in a concern to treat most issues in terms of the family. One of the primary concerns of social work is to patch up marital conflicts and tensions so that family relationships may be restored to a working equilibrium – usually for the sake of the children. Additionally, whereas social workers have no statutory responsibilities to deal with adults, they can legally be called to account for their child care provision. Our early contact with the department whose files we investigated emphasised the voluntary nature of their help to battered women as opposed to their statutory responsibilities for children. This was very obviously reflected both in the ways in which domestic violence was dealt with and in the issues which social workers saw as being most urgently in need of attention. An analysis of the files reveals that only three of the twenty-six battering cases we analysed were regarded as being centrally in any way about battering. Only in these three cases does the social worker feel under any obligation to visit because the man is violent to the woman. The main concern of most of the other cases is with the welfare of the children. In eighteen cases where systematic violence is being committed by the man in the home, the apparent interest of the social worker lies either in the particular problems of individual children (for example behaviour problems, truancy, theft), or the general standard of child care in the home, or in making sure that the children are not being affected by the man's aggression towards the woman. On any number of occasions the social worker will ask the woman if he ill-treats the children. The files continually record such concern: 'My major concern is for the children's future.' 'The most distressing aspect of these upheavals are that they are often in front of the children.' 'And although he beats his wife frequently he rarely hits the children.' It could be that the files do not record the emotional sympathy given by the social workers to the women. This we can never know. The emphasis upon areas for which they are legally responsible may be the result of social workers' desire to put on record the fact that this *is* their primary concern. But it is hard to escape the conclusion that these professional duties and responsibilities, together with a stance which denies partisanship, has, as its consequence, a response to the plight of battered women which smacks heavily of callous indifference.

Social workers, wife beating and mental health

Despite the individuality of the cases and the involvement of different social workers, the conclusions of the files seemed to follow a similar predictable pattern – a pattern involving depression, commital to mental institutions and even attempted suicide. Twelve of the women are referred to in the files as being 'depressed' and feelings of lethargy and lack of energy are mentioned so frequently as to defy quantification: 'But with her apathy and depression, it was almost as if she had a death wish about her.' 'She continued to present herself as lethargic and depressed.' More dramatically, two of the women threatened to commit suicide on a number of occasions and five of them actually attempted to kill themselves. Furthermore ten of the women received in-patient treatment in mental hospitals. (Given our one in ten sample of all files, this implies a figure of 100.) One woman was deemed to require such treatment but refused to go.

The recording of the process leading up to a woman's commital to mental institutions and the diagnoses involved markedly lacked the detailed descriptions which typify some of the other file entries we have looked at. It seems sufficient to record on the files that the woman has been 'admitted' with no further elaboration required. There is little attempt to record the connections between the instances of battering, the social conditions in which the women live, and the onset of depression or other forms of mental anguish. Indeed no comment is made regarding the fact that although it is the men who commit the violence, it is the women who have to bear the psychological pain and hospitalisation. At its most stark, many of the cases we examined seemed to be examples of blaming the victim since it is the women, not the men, who are defined as inadequate and unable to cope. The family circumstances seem to be regarded as immutable and therefore devoid of blame or remedy. Additionally, little is said, by way of diagnosis, about the emotional consequences of finding oneself a 'battered woman' – not, one would suggest, an insignificant change of status for the women concerned.[6]

Why the social worker indifference?

Having completed our analysis of social worker responses to wives who had been beaten, the next most obvious step was to explain such responses. Why do social workers apparently show such little interest in battered women? Why is it that one of the most prominent of the so-called 'caring professions' seems to care so little in this instance? It was clear from the considerable evidence contained in the files that part of such an explanation lies in the attitudes that social workers have towards women as clients, their images of women who are battered and their reasoning as to why husbands beat wives. It has already been mentioned that in only three of the wife-beating cases we discussed was battering recognised as a central concern. Of the others, the vast majority had children's and family welfare as their main focus. In this context there was a paradox in the way that social workers dealt with their female clients. Whatever the nature of the presenting problem, social workers regarded the woman in her role as wife/mother as their primary contact. It was the wife/mother they expected to visit and with whom they envisaged discussing the issues at hand. On the very few occasions when the man only was available at the time of a particular visit, the social worker remarked on the wife's absence as something strange, emphasising the importance of her being part of the case. In none of the many cases where the man is never or seldom seen does the social worker remark on this or indicate that his presence might be relevant or helpful. It seems that when a problem relates to the family or children, social workers regard the wife/mother only as being centrally involved. Family matters are *her* matters and any problems are for *her* to resolve. However, and here the paradox appears, although the woman is seen as the fundamental member of the family, she is seldom treated as an individual. Little sympathy is given to her particular problems, unless they can be seen to be affecting other family members. Indeed she is frequently encouraged to suppress her own fears and emotions for the sake of these others. Women are treated as appendages of their families rather than as individuals in their own right.

Where social workers do appear to take notice of the women in these battering cases, it is with regard to the adequate fulfilling of their 'normal' domestic duties. Nowhere are such duties defined, but it is quite clear that an implicit view of what constitutes 'normality' underlies the assessment of their female clients. Moreover, social workers seem acutely conscious of any deviations from this 'normality'. Descriptions of the woman's domestic and personal inadequacies comprise a major way in which they feature in the files: (social worker visits because the woman has been beaten) 'House is in a shocking condition. I insisted she should get it cleaned up before I called again.' 'She always has full make-up on but the house was in a tip.' Such women are being judged not only in terms of their personal appearance but on the appearance of their homes. The judgment is that their performances in these areas are indicative of their failure and inadequacies as persons. This view of personal and domestic incompetence is crucial for an understanding of social workers' lack of response to beaten wives. In a brief analysis of both the reasons behind the marital tension and the specific triggers to a particular violent incident, the man's complaints about his wife's performance of housewifely duties was overwhelmingly the most significant grievance stated. For example: 'She never does any housework or cooks a meal. Mr Blank describes her household management as appalling.' 'She is not overactive in household duties. Her husband complains of her neglect of him and the children.' These statements are presented on the files as part of the social worker's explanation as to why violence should occur. They are reported as having been offered to them by the men in response to requests for such explanations. Sex was also a source of conflict: 'Apart from domestic incompetence, she is also failing to meet his sexual demands.'

I am not concerned as to whether such complaints are 'true' or not. What is significant is the way that social workers appear to implicitly accept such complaints as reasons for the ensuing physical assaults. The entries on the files imply that in these statements we have 'understandable' accounts of how aggression occurs. Social workers, as we have seen, regard women as adjuncts of their families. But to be a successful adjunct involves the adequate fulfilment of traditional wifely duties – especially those of housekeeping and sex. It seems that if the woman is somehow deviant in the ways she looks after herself, her husband and her home, then social workers feel they can understand, although not of course condone, his subsequent violent action. They are indirectly suggesting that a man's natural need for satisfactory domestic and sexual arrangements can equally naturally lead to drinking, violence, and temper, when he does not have these so-called needs fulfilled. The man can then claim that he lost control or was not himself and the social worker audience will be able to understand his behaviour, although they may not excuse it. For instance, one file records: 'Tony talked of his temper and not being able to control it.'

It appears from the files that social workers collude with the man in seeing domestic failings as comprehendable reasons for violence. I am not suggesting that such violence is regarded as a legitimate way of expressing one's feelings but that it is regarded as an almost rational response to certain failings on the woman's part. Thus social workers implied that the violence was 'natural in the circumstances'. They tried to persuade the woman to please her man, particularly by avoiding challenging him, as the best defence against being beaten up. For instance, 'It is most important that this couple stick together for the sake of the children and I think this could be achieved more safely by encouraging Mrs Blank to accept her husband's decisions.' There is something slightly strange about this and other statements. Somehow it is being suggested that the women, the victims, should take on some kind of responsibility for pacifying the husband's aggression. The impression is given that the wives will be able to influence their husband's behaviour, through certain kinds of reticence on their part. They are responsible not only for the family and the children, but also for their man's responses to the family situation. It is the woman who has to make amends. Such a view only makes sense if the woman is regarded as being implicated in the man's violence. Behind such advice hides the insinuation that the women themselves have instigated a battering through some kind of inciteful action. This stance of blaming the victim is not just an implicit response that social workers make to wife beating. The idea that the women provoke their husbands' violence is explicitly stated on the files: 'It seems her nagging is the trigger for his violence.' 'I feel she could be provoking his violence towards her.'

In addition to victim blaming, social workers were also suspicious that the women didn't really tell them the truth. This also provides a ready-made justification for inaction: 'Mrs Blank appears to have to complain about something . . . I wonder if she feels she has to produce some problem because a social worker visits.' 'I am not a hundred per cent sure that Mrs Blank is telling the truth.'

The entries on the files regarding victim blaming and

questioning what the woman say are made alongside detailed recordings of the beatings women have suffered. This appears to be rather dissonant. Are we really to believe that social workers think being beaten with a shillelagh, punched and kneed is a justifiable or reasonable response to 'nagging', or that a client is making up a problem when only the week previously her cohabitee has broken her head open with a gun? The files suggest that they can tolerate such inconsistencies. Sometimes the suggestion is that the woman enjoys 'it': 'There is an element of satisfaction . . . in the way she describes her treatment in his hands.' Sometimes inactivity is sanctioned by the supposed acceptance of the violence by the woman: 'She complains he hits her. This is also accepted by her.' Or sometimes the social workers' inactivity in the face of wife beating is explained away as the natural assertion of dominance by the man over the woman: 'Mr Blank apparently likes to dominate his wife, probably to compensate for her inabilities and in spite of her complaints this is probably what the wife responds to.'

It is clear that the majority of social workers whose case files we read were uninterested in their battered women clients, except where they could be reprimanded for poor housekeeping and personal appearances. It is obvious too that these social workers operated with an implicit view of what would comprise failing in one's wifely duties and that this was substantially in agreement with the views of the husbands. It therefore becomes possible for social workers to see domestic violence as rational, if not legitimate, aggression, when it is used to chastise a wayward wife. Such a view is compounded if one believes that a woman is apt to provoke a husband to violence or that she may well be untruthful in the various claims she makes about the extent of the violence and its consequences. All these provide grounds for social workers to be indifferent, inactive and unresponsive to women in battering cases.

Conclusion

The main purpose of this chapter has been to document and illustrate the ways in which social workers deal, or rather do not deal, with the wife beating found in their day-to-day casework as recorded on case files. It has attempted to uncover the beliefs, assumptions and attitudes which seem to underlie social worker practice in relation to battered women and the accompanying lack of sympathy towards the victim. From our analysis of files the most obvious preconceptions can be itemised as follows:

(1) A tendency to regard any housewifely or wifely deviation (from an unspecified norm) as evidence of the woman's inadequacy or inability to cope with and perform her duties properly. This means that any breakdown within the family becomes the *woman's* own private problem which she must rectify, rather than the problem of her situation or others within that situation.

(2) A disinclination to believe what battered women say about their domestic situation. This is usually a consequence of their supposed immaturity, inadequacy and the derogatory comments of the man.

(3) Tacitly supporting the nuclear family structure and the inferior position of the woman within it. This occurs through social workers doing nothing that might be seen to threaten the survival of a particular family unit. Their concern is to restore a domestic equilibrium, even where battering is still occurring, although this might be seen to operate against the best interests of the woman involved.

(4) Offering tacit support to male domination and control of women by supporting, implicitly, male reasons for violence and encouraging women to understand and respond to these reasons.

I do not wish to be seen here as criticising individual social workers. Rather it is the systematic patterning and repetition of assumptions and associated practices that should be emphasised. It is not that particular social workers necessarily have malicious attitudes towards battered women, but rather that social work's professional self-image, its training programmes and its definitional duties as laid down by the state, preclude the likelihood of being sympathetically active in dealing with wife beating.[7] Thus we are dealing here with a set of preconceptions which give a specific shape to social work practice and enable social workers to ignore certain parts of a case and rationalise away as insignificant what others might well regard as the central and most pressing issue. We are in fact referring to an 'ideology of social work'.[8]

We should not be surprised that these assumptive and diagnostic definitions of reality are so readily visible as constitutive of the ideological basis of social worker practice. Ideologies, after all, are based upon beliefs and interpretations which purport to be true or valid. They should not be understood in terms of what is hidden and concealed 'but precisely what is most open, apparent and manifest'.[9] Ideology operates on the surface and in view of us all. By contrast what is hidden or repressed are its real foundations. It is these aspects which are unconscious and concealed.[10] Furthermore, the *power* of ideologies is related to the way in which they are used to justify and legitimise actions. Ideological views of the world are regarded by those who hold them as 'self-evident', 'realistic' or 'based on what human nature is'. In each case an ideology is being used to determine what counts as 'realistic' action and to define the limits of 'rational' choice.[11] It seems to me that social work ideologies function in just such a way. They comprise a set of views relating, for example, to wives who are beaten and the nature of family life, which set limits upon what social workers see as being realistic or reasonable action for them to take. Such ideologies provide a language that allows interpretations to be made of things seen and heard within the immediacy of everyday life.[12] Moreover the inevitable consequence of the social worker practices described here is to re-emphasise those norms of privacy and particularly isolation discussed briefly at the beginning of this chapter. One of the by-products of the increased importance afforded to individuality and privacy has been the growth of the new industry of counselling services, catering for the proliferation of personal troubles that seem to erupt from our privatised form of family life. Social work, of course, forms a significant part of this development. In emphasising that family problems are solvable in individual terms, social work helps to strengthen the status of the private. It encourages clients to see problems as *their* problems only and to adapt to their privatised situation. Paradoxically then the social worker's 'intrusion' into the privacy of the family ultimately serves to reinforce that privacy. For women who are battered it supports the explanation of wife beating in terms of individual pathology and hence increases the isolation that they are already experiencing. But it would of course be nonsense to see the attitudes and sentiments I have described as being the sole prerogative of social workers. Social work ideology is not an isolated and autonomous system of belief but is premised upon the ideology of wider society. In this context I would like, finally, to raise two related issues.

Firstly, what I have been discussing can be considered as an instance of the mechanism of patriarchy. Social work ideology as outlined above is one particular manifestation of patriarchal ideology. In general terms, patriarchy refers to male domination and to the power relationships by which men dominate women.[13] Feminists have recently been trying to come to grips with the term patriarchy, when for a long time it had usually been invoked by way of explanation rather than being analysed in itself. Despite its undoubted value, the work that has so far been produced has been fairly abstract. There still seems to be a gap between theorising about patriarchy and what we commonsensically know as women, through our own experiences. My suggestion is that throughout this paper patriarchy is being described. Patriarchy is not some kind of 'out there', reified, external structure but an ongoing day-to-day activity. Patriarchy does not hover above everyday life; it *is* everyday life. Social work ideology, together with its various practices, is just one instance of the many, many ways in which the structures of patriarchy are upheld and men's subordination of women on a social, sexual and economic level maintained.

Secondly, in order to be able to discuss more fully and in greater depth the nature of patriarchy, how it works and operates, and its consequences, we need to undertake more direct and detailed empirical work. There is not *one* patriarchal ideology. Rather, there are many interrelated ways of maintaining the structure of male domination and control. These need to be investigated and their relationship displayed, at the same time as we are discussing patriarchy as a more theoretical concept. By looking, especially, at circumscribed areas of social life but in particular at agencies of the state, we can begin to develop a picture of the complexity of the patriarchal network. In this study of social workers we can see how their treatment of male violence against women constitutes a working patriarchy. It is apparent that social work, part of the so-called caring arm of the state, differs hardly at all from other state agencies in terms of the views of women which it holds. It is perhaps not too much to suggest that this case study of social workers' response to domestic violence illustrates how the state upholds male domination, control and the policing of women.

Notes

I am very grateful to Bob Coles for all his help and encouragement in the analysis of the research data and the preparation of this chapter.

1   Although I use the term wife beating, the violence described on the social work files occurred within cohabiting as well as marriage relationships. As R. Emerson Dobash and Russell Dobash have pointed out in *Violence Against Wives*, Shepton Mallet, Open Books, 1980, the term wife beating emphasises the fact that it is the husband who is likely to be the aggressor and his wife the victim, and that the violence takes place in the family setting.

2   For example, Eli Zaretsky, *Capitalism, the Family and Personal Life*, London, Pluto Press, 1976; Ann Oakley, *The Sociology of Housework*, Oxford, Martin Robertson, 1974; Arthur Brittan, *The Privatised World*, London, Routledge & Kegan Paul, 1977.

3   Dobash and Dobash, op. cit.

4   The research was originated by Bob Coles, Judy Nixon and Pat Young and carried out by Bob Coles, Pat Young and myself, although the responsibility for the analysis of the information collected is entirely mine. The area covered by the research included both rural and urban districts, the urban comprising a population of more than 100,000.

5   The surname Blank has been used for all clients and their forenames changed to ensure anonymity.

6   A classic study of depression amongst women suggests that status change is an important trigger to the onset of depression, although becoming a battered wife does not figure amongst the status changes discussed in the book. See George W. Brown and Tirril Harris, *Social Origins of Depression*, London, Tavistock Publications, 1978.

7   I am grateful to Jo Sutton and Jalna Hanmer for drawing my attention to this point.

8 The very use of the term ideology is fraught with difficulties. There is a tendency for it to be used in a cavalier and rhetorical way which merely denotes that the beliefs it encompasses are in some way wrong or misconceived. There is also a far more specific meaning derived from the works of Karl Marx and rooted in an analysis of class society. There is no space to explore these highly complicated debates here, although as feminists we need to clarify how we wish to use the term.

9 Stuart Hall, 'Culture, the media and the "ideological effect" ', in James Curran *et al.* (eds), *Mass Communication and Society*, London, Open University Press, 1977.

10 Stuart Hall, op. cit.

11 Richard J. Bernstein, *The Restructuring of Social and Political theory*, Oxford, Basil Blackwell, 1976.

12 Alvin Gouldner, *The Dialectics of Ideology and Technology*, London, Macmillan, 1976, 42.

13 For an analysis of the various ways in which feminists have used the term patriarchy see Veronica Beechey, 'On patriarchy', *Feminist Review*, no. 3, 1979.

Chapter ten

The contact between battered women and social and medical agencies

R. Emerson Dobash, Russell P. Dobash
and Katherine Cavanagh

The battered woman's need for assistance from others, like the violence she experiences, begins early in the marital or cohabiting relationship and continues to change over time as the man's violence grows more frequent and severe and the woman actively seeks a cessation to it.[1] Throughout this process, a dynamic pattern develops which includes: the violence itself, the couple's overall relationship, the woman's contact with outsiders and the responses of those contacted. Violence, contacts and responses become inextricably intertwined in the unfolding of the problem.

We will examine the patterns of help seeking behaviour as they change over time and as they are related both to the severity of the violence and to the response of those approached for assistance. Using the data from systematic indepth interviews with 109 battered women[2] we will delineate the emergence and continuation of the violence, examine its severity and relationship to help seeking behaviour, and analyse the point of contact between battered women and others, particularly social workers and the medical profession. In brief, the evidence shows that: (1) the violence enters the relationship early and increases in frequency and severity over time; (2) the act of seeking help from others is not solely related to the severity of a specific violent attack; (3) help-seeking behaviour is mediated through a number of social, moral and material factors relating to the woman's position as wife and mother within a patriarchical family structure; and (4) the nature of women's requests for help and the types of responses received from professionals and others change over time.

The violence

The woman's need for social and medical services, or any service for that matter, is predicated upon the emergence and continuation of the man's violent behaviour. One of the most striking features about the nature of the violence, is its early appearance in the relationship. It can be seen in Table 10.1 that half of the women were assaulted within the first year of marriage or cohabitation and there were very few cases in which the violence emerged after the first three years. Once the violence began, it could go on for many years unless the man could be stopped, an unlikely prospect under current circumstances, or the woman could find a means of escaping from the relationship. For example, it can be seen in Table 10.2 that although the violence usually entered the relationship within the first year or two, the majority of women suffered it for many years before they found refuge with Women's Aid. In addition to the number of years the violence continued, there was also the frequency with which such attacks occurred, and for most of these women, this eventually meant approximately two attacks each week.[3]

The nature of the violence itself was also quite diverse and changed over time (Dobash *et al.*, 1978; Dobash and Dobash, 1979; 1983). In order to obtain detailed information about the violence we asked the women about three specific events, the *first*, the *worst* and the *last* before leaving to seek refuge. The

Table 10.1: Length of marriage or cohabitation at time of first assault

Year	N	%
Before marriage or cohabitation	21	20
1	50	47
2	10	9
3	11	10
4	5	5
5 and over	9	9
Total	106*	100

* *3 cases missing*

Table 10.2: Length of marriage or cohabitation when woman sought refuge

Year	N	%
1	5	5
2	9	8
2-5	23	21
5-10	33	30
10-15	18	16
15-20	15	14
20+	6	6
Total	109	100

three specific episodes were considered in order to examine three time periods in the relationship and the extreme point of violence. These accounts covered numerous aspects of the events including the nature of the argument, the forms of physical attack, the nature of injuries, immediate and long-term responses to the violence and contact with third parties in search of assistance. In addition, the same information was gathered about the *typical* assault. This was done in order to provide information about the majority of violent events experienced by the women and to overcome the possibility that the three specific events may have been unique. These accounts reveal that the *first* attack usually involved slapping or punching and resulted in bruises and cuts. As the violence continued, its intensity and severity increased. The *worst, last* and *typical* assaults described by the women usually involved slapping, punching, pushing into injurious objects (e.g. tables or walls), and kicking and butting. Some men also stood or jumped on their wives and/or attempted to strangle or drown them. One of the most usual patterns was for the man to push or punch the woman to the floor and then proceed to kick and punch her. Attacks such as these resulted in numerous injuries. For example, extensive bruises and cuts of the face, limbs and body were very common while fractured bones and teeth, severe burns, internal injuries and miscarriages also occurred. In addition, many women suffered from chronic emotional distress.

Overall, the data reveal that women experienced violence early in their relationshp and that its frequency and severity increased over time, making it a constant reality of their daily lives. Research from several countries reveals similar patterns. That is, wives are the most likely family members to be subjected to severe, persistent and continual violence, and these attacks often result in severe injuries (Gelles, 1974; Martin, 1976; Gaguin, 1978; Pahl, 1978; Dobash and Dobash, 1978; 1979; 1981a; Pagelow, 1981).

Severity of violence and help seeking

It is this violence, along with continual intimidation, coercion and threats that constitute the background against which women seek assistance. It is often assumed that there is, or should be, a direct correspondence between the severity of violence and both the seeking of help and the provision of assistance.[4] Among many, there is the implicit idea that the severity of a given attack is related to whether or not a woman seeks assistance and from whom it is sought. Speculative notions about the severity of violence are sometimes used in deciding whether a woman is 'truly' battered or whether a particular incident is violent enough to warrant assistance. Because of the pervasiveness and importance of these notions, we will examine the severity of violence and help-seeking behaviour using data from detailed accounts of 314 specific violent episodes. These represent the *first, worst* and *last* violent events experienced by each of the 109 women interviewed.[5] In addition, information about the *typical* form of attack experienced by the 109 women has also been included. Before considering the relationship between the severity of violence and help-seeking behaviour, we will first consider separately our measurement of severity of violence and some of the general patterns of help seeking.

In order to summarise and compare violent events, a Severity of Violence Scale was constructed. The scale included specific information about each incident, including: (1) the types of physical attack (e.g. kick, hit, butt); (2) the types of injuries inflicted (e.g. bruise, burn, fracture); and (3) the number of different types of injuries sustained (Cavanagh,

1978). For each violent incident, the first two factors, types of physical attack and types of injury, were given a weighting of increasing severity and summated. These two scores were then added to the third, number of injuries, giving an overall severity score for each violent incident, e.g. the *first, worst, last* and *typical*.[6] When this process was completed, the results were divided into four categories of severity: low, medium, high and extreme. These multidimensional scores were developed using an interactive method in which conceptual categories, empirical data and verbatim accounts were constantly worked and checked in relation to one another.[7]

Table 10.3 presents the severity of the *typical* assaults experienced by the women. It can be seen that a very small percentage (3 per cent) were assessed as low in severity, while almost half (46 per cent) were of medium severity and the other half (51 per cent) were scored as high or extreme. Information about the *typical* assault, although based on descriptions of what an episode was usually like rather than upon an account of a specific episode, provides us with an indicator of the degree of severity of the majority of violent events experienced by the women and dispels the all-too-common belief that such incidents involve just the odd slap.

Table 10.3: Degree of the severity of a typical assault

	N	%
Low	3	3
Medium	50	46
High	54	49
Extreme	2	2
TOTAL	109	100

Patterns of help-seeking behaviour

Although the literature on help-seeking behaviour is fairly extensive, little research has been conducted on patterns of help seeking among women who have experienced persistent violence. However, this general literature provides a useful background for research on battered women. A recent review of this literature has classified the majority of the work as focusing either upon the individual client or upon wider contextual factors (Brannen, 1980). The individual approach usually focuses on personal or psychological characteristics of clients, decision-making processes and/or knowledge and perception of services (Glastonbury, Burdett and Austen, 1973), while the contextual approach usually focuses on the social situation surrounding the client and the role of the agencies themselves (Greenley and Mechanic, 1976). In addition, there has been some work which uses a more interactive perspective and focuses both on the client and her relationship with the social agency (Mayer and Timms, 1970). Despite the diversity of approaches, the results of this research reveal that prospective clients usually have little knowledge about social agencies and many have negative conceptions about such agencies that lead to a reluctance to make and/or sustain contact (Levinger, 1960; Cartwright, 1967; Weiss, 1973; Reith, 1975; Giordano, 1977). Overcoming this reluctance is very difficult and is often affected by several factors including myth and rumour about the agency, the orientation and support of friends and relatives and the response of the agencies themselves (Nichols, 1976; Giordano, 1977; Pahl, 1979b; Brannen, 1980).

The findings from our research also show this general reluctance to make contact either with informal sources such as relatives, friends or neighbours or with formal sources such as doctors, social workers and the police. For example, we found that less than 2 per cent of all the violent assaults ever experienced were reported to the police. Despite this reluctance to report the vast majority of assaults experienced, most of the women did make some form of contact on at least one or more occasions. Table 10.4 reveals that very few women remained completely silent about the violence. Instead, an extremely large proportion made initial attempts to seek assistance from a wide variety of third parties. Whether they continued to pursue such assistance often depended upon the response they received and the perceived effect the contact had upon the cessation, continuation or escalation of the man's violent behaviour.

Table 10.4: Number of women contacting third parties at least once throughout the violent relationship

	N	%
Informal:		
Relatives	83	76
Friends	53	49
Neighbours	47	43
Formal:		
Doctor	87	80
Social Worker	81	74
Police	89	82
Minister	26	24
Other	49	45

N = 109

Table 10.5: Number of contacts made by women after each assault

Number Contacts	First		Assault Worst		Last	
	N	%	N	%	N	%
0	54	51	12	12	3	3
1-2	34	32	35	45	32	29
3-4	15	14	30	30	53	49
5-6	3	3	13	13	20	20
Total	106[1]	100	100[2,3]	100	108[4]	101*

* rounding
N = 109
Gamma (γ) = 0.54
1 Three women could not recall first assault
2 Eight 'test' interviews did not include a worst assault
3 One woman could not distinguish a worst assault from the others because of persistent severity
4 One woman had suffered verbal and psychological abuse rather than physical abuse during the last two years of marriage.

The nature and number of contacts made in search of assistance changed over time. Table 10.5 reveals a distinct increase in the number of contacts made from the *first* to the *last* attack. After the *first* attack, about half of the women (49 per cent) made one or more contacts with outsiders. This increased to 88 per cent after the *worst* and 97 per cent after the *last* attack. These data indicate that women do seek help, and that they do so much more frequently as the violence continues. Using Gamma (Mueller, Schussler and Costner, 1970) to assess the degree of association between the two ordinal level variables reveals quite a strong association between the continuation of violence and the number of contacts made (Gamma = 0.54). That is, the longer the violence continues in the relationship the greater the number of contacts that are made in efforts to deal with it.

Table 10.6: Type of contacts made after each assault

| Type of contact | | | Assault | | | | |
| | First | | Worst | | | Last | |
	N	%	N	%		N	%
Informal:							
Relatives	37	33	47	19		42	10
Friends	20	18	20	8		33	9
Neighbours	13	11	24	10		23	6
Formal:							
Doctors	21	18	53	22		43	12
Social Worker	6	5	35	14		63	17
Police	12	11	35	14		47	13
Other	4	4	18	7		27	7
Women's Aid*	0	0	14	6		93	25
Total contacts	113	100	246	100		371	100
No. Women making no contacts	52		88			105	

Women's Aid is an artifact of the sample, but is included to show overall pattern of usage for the sample
Ref: Dobash and Dobash (1979)

The changing nature of contacts is also apparent in the type of third party from whom assistance was sought. Table 10.6 shows that those women who did make some type of contact after the first assault were most likely to go to informal sources, particularly relatives. As the violence persisted they continued to use informal sources quite heavily but increasingly approached formal sources, particularly doctors, social workers and the police.

Our findings show that the reasons for this changing pattern of contacts are complex and relate to a number of factors that vary during the relationship. For example, after the *first* attack, the women generally felt that they did not need assistance. They believed the attack to be a unique event, which it was at the time, and that their husband would never do it again. At this stage, there was still considerable hope for the future of the relationship and little reason to believe that it would be anything other than non-violent. As one woman remarked about the first assault, 'It never entered my head to go to anybody for help. I didn't need it. It was just an accident that could have happened to anyone at any time.' The men sometimes reinforced this evaluation, particularly after the first few attacks, by behaving in a contrite and apologetic manner and promising to reform. However, these evaluations, the woman's predicament and the orientation and behaviour of the man changed dramatically as the violence continued.

To summarise, there are several major patterns of help-seeking behaviour evident in these data. Firstly, the number of women who make some form of contact with others increases over time, from approximately half the women after the *first* assault to almost all of them after the *last*. This demonstrates an increase in the active attempts of women to approach others in their efforts to stop the violence or escape from it. Secondly, relatives are the most likely to be contacted after the *first* assault and the number of women making contact with relatives and friends continues to be high over time. Thirdly, there is a shift in the type of contacts made as the violence continues and worsens. Although the number of women contacting informal sources continues at a fairly steady state, the number of women making contact with formal agencies increases fairly substantially with the *worst* and *last* assaults.

It should be noted, however, that because of the nature of the worst and last assaults, it would be expected that more women might draw upon the services of relevant social agencies on these occasions. However, the general pattern still indicates that most women who seek assistance from statutory, social or medical agencies will most likely have sought assistance from relatives and friends for some time prior to seeking professional assistance.

The relationship between severity of violence and help-seeking behaviour

A complex and changing relationship between the severity of violence and help-seeking behaviour is revealed in Tables 10.7 and 10.8. However, the relationship between these two factors must be considered relative to the fact that there is a general increase both in the number of contacts made over time and in the proportion of events that are more severe. It must be stressed that this overall pattern of increasing severity and increasing number of contacts over time cannot be taken to mean that a direct relationship necessarily exists between them for any specific attack. Therefore, in order to assess the relationship between the severity of a particular violent event and the number of contacts made after it, these factors were examined *within* violent assaults rather than *across* these episodes.

In Table 10.7 a Gamma of .50 reveals a relatively strong relationship between the severity of the *first* assault and the number of contacts made with outsiders. That is, for the *first* assault, greater severity of violence is associated with a greater number of contacts. In contrast, a Gamma of −.07 in Table 10.8 indicates that no such relationship exists between the severity of the *worst* assault and contact with outsiders. In other words, high or extreme severity of violence is associated with seeking assistance from several sources after the *first* assault but not after the *worst* assault. These results indicate that the severity of a particular violent event is not the only or possibly even the major factor associated with the amount of help seeking following that event.

Table 10.7: Number of contacts made with various sources of help in relation to the degree of severity of the first assault

Degree of Severity	Number of Contacts				
	0	1-2	3-4	5+	Total
Low	38	15	3	1	57
Medium	11	11	7	1	30
High	5	6	5	1	17
Extreme	0	2	0	0	2
Total	54	34	15	3	106

Gamma $(\gamma) = .50$

Table 10.8: Number of contacts made with various sources of help in relation to the degree of severity of the worst assault

Degree of Severity	Number of Contacts				
	0	1-2	3-4	5+	Total
Low	0	3	3	1	7
Medium	5	15	11	4	35
High	5	19	13	6	43
Extreme	2	8	3	2	15
Total	12	45	30	13	100

Gamma $(\gamma) = -.07$

Impediments to help seeking

Given these findings, additional analysis is necessary to explain why women do or do not seek help. This involves factors associated with the women, the men and the formal agencies. For the women, one of the most important mechanisms inhibiting help seeking was the shame and guilt associated with the violence. Widely held beliefs about domestic privacy and autonomy, respectability and the notion that marital happiness and stability are the primary respons- ibility of women create feelings of responsibility for domestic problems. In the personal context, violence often serves as an indicator to the woman that she has somehow 'failed', resulting in feelings of shame and guilt. For the violence to become public knowledge adds to this as personal 'failure' is translated into public stigma.

> I felt very ashamed, very very ashamed, more ashamed
> than anything else and I certainly wouldn't let it be
> known to anybody, particularly my mother or the
> neighbours because I was supposed to be married and
> happy and to tell anybody would be nasty.

Since the family is perceived to be a private domain, it can be seen as an offence to breach that privacy no matter how extreme the misbehaviour of any family member. The women indicated that their husbands often reinforced such ideals about privacy and contributed to their sense of shame. This was done first by blaming the women for 'provoking' the violence and then by maintaining that she deserved still more if she violated *his* privacy by seeking assistance from others. In addition, patriarchal relationships are based upon beliefs in trust and loyalty from subordinates, and to seek outside help is a betrayal of that tacit bond of loyalty. This coercion of the conscience is a powerful mechanism in the arsenal of male domination. A woman commits a double affront when she breaks this moral suasion, that is, betrayal of loyalty to her husband and exposure of his behaviour and their relationship to public scrutiny.

Such social and moral restraints were often accompanied by more direct physical barriers such as forcible confinement in the house and threatened reprisals:

> 'I wasn't allowed to a telephone box to phone the police
> or anybody. I wasn't allowed to get to the bleeding door,
> let alone the police.'

> 'I never went to anybody. I couldn't go to my doctor
> because he threatened me that if I went to the doctor I
> might as well not come back because it would get worse.'

Such threats were more likely when intended approaches were to formal agencies rather than informal acquaintances, perhaps because men were more concerned about the authority and potential sanctions of professionals.

Despite these obstacles, women certainly contemplated seeking assistance from formal agencies. But, as with those who seek help for other types of problems, these deliberations were sometimes based on little knowledge of the agencies and considerable concern about the nature of the response. For example, one woman told us: 'I knew about the social work. I knew they existed but not for this type of thing. To me the social work was for families and homeless and things like that.' Many women were afraid to seek help because they feared a negative response: 'My doctor's not the kind to give help or advice so I knew it was useless going to him. He was a man anyway and he would probably have sympathised with John [husband].' Some women did not wish to contact an agency because they thought professionals would intrude too much on their family life and/or increase the stigma: 'I felt that when you get in tow with these people [social workers] they interfere too much in your home life and with your kids, and the running of your house, which I didn't think was necessary.'

The woman's sense of isolation, shame and guilt, the husband's justifications and threats and the concerns about agency response did not, of course, completely prevent women from seeking help. However, they did contribute to ambivalence and reticence in making and maintaining contact. Over time, as the frequency and intensity of the violence increased, many of these impediments became less powerful and women sought more assistance.

> 'In the beginning I would never go down to the shops in case anybody would see my face but after that last time I thought, "Why should I feel ashamed? I've done nothing." I went out and let everybody see what he had done to me.'

Evaluations such as these are extremely significant in the decision to seek more or different types of assistance. Indeed, it is important for professionals to recognise that it may not be the severity of a particular attack that leads a woman to seek help. Rather, it may be the cumulative effect of persistent violence and intimidation, decreasing acceptance of the man's justifications for violence and repeated failures to solve the problem alone. Even then, the decision to approach a formal agency is a very difficult one. The initial contact is so fraught with misgivings and trepidation that the nature of the response can easily lead to discontinuation of contact.

Contact with formal agencies: requests and responses

Despite all of the difficulties, most of the women in our study eventually made a wide variety of contacts with third parties in their efforts to eliminate the man's violent behaviour. It is at this point of contact that we might examine the changing nature of the type of requests made and the responses received, as well as the degree of challenge each poses to the violence itself and to its social and ideological supports.

There were at least four general types of requests for assistance made by the women. They included: requesting assistance in stopping a particular attack; seeking a sympathetic person to listen and give moral, medical or material support after an attack; trying to involve others in the ongoing negotiations with the man in order to stop the continuing violence; and, finally, attempting to gain the material assistance, such as accommodation and financial support, necessary to escape from a violent relationship. Although the particular requests varied in nature, they were all oriented in some way to the woman's attempts to stop the violence. An analytical examination of these requests reveals that they all contain elements that are supportive of the woman, but only some embody more direct and explicit challenges to the violence and/or its social underpinnings. For example, a woman may seek someone with whom she might discuss the violence in the hope that this will somehow help her find a means of solving the problem. By doing so, the woman may certainly receive much needed moral support and a lessening of her isolation but unless something else is actually done, sympathetic listening alone will not provide a direct challenge to the violence in any of its forms (i.e. a particular violent attack, the man's ongoing violent behaviour, the continuation of a violent relationship or the social relations that underpin and support wife beating in general). Requests that embodied challenges to the violence included attempts to gain assistance in stopping or escaping from a violent episode or from the violent relationship itself.

Requests for assistance form only part of the dynamic process of eliminating violence. It is also shaped by the nature of the response which may also be seen as more or less challenging the violence. In order to analyse this dynamic process, we characterised the responses as either supportive of the woman or challenging the violence. By supportive responses we are referring to those responses where, for example, the woman seeks a sympathetic listener and is heard, given credence and treated sympathetically, but no attempts are made to confront the violence itself. Challenging responses include such things as advising the woman about her rights and assisting her in acquiring them, attempting to stop an attack in progress, speaking to the man about the unacceptability of the violence, referring to agencies and assisting the woman to escape from violence. Where the response was both supportive and challenging, it was defined as challenging. Although these two general characterisations were sufficient to define the requests, they were not sufficient for the responses. They included a third type, negative actions such as denial, negation, victim blaming and refusal to assist.

It can be seen in Table 10.9 that the nature of the requests made by the 109 women changed over time from those that

Table 10.9: Nature of help requested by women after each assault (in percentages)

Request	Assault			
	First	Worst	Last	
Supportive	73	58	34	
Challenging	27	42	66	
Total	100	100	100	
No. contacts	113	246	371	730

were mostly supportive to those that were mostly challenging. For example, after the *first* assault a total of 113 contacts were made with third parties; of these, 73 per cent were requests for supportive forms of assistance. By comparison, a total of 371 contacts were made after the *last* assault and 66 per cent of them were for challenging forms of assistance.

The nature of the responses to these two general types of requests were diverse, ranging from attempts to minimise, deny or ignore them to active attempts to meet even the most challenging. Of course, the nature of the response must be seen relative to the type of request made and the person to whom it was put. For example, relatives, particularly parents, were usually asked for both supportive and challenging types of assistance. Supportive requests were almost always responded to positively, and challenging ones, especially requests for temporary accommodation that would allow escape from the husband for a few days, were usually met, although certainly not always. Refusals were not usually determined so much by the willingness to offer tangible assistance as by the problematic material circumstances that limited the ability to provide help.

> 'My parents were more than willing to take me but my father was dying of cancer and I couldn't possibly inflict myself and the kids on them.'

> 'I never wanted to go back but I was forced into it because me and the kids staying with Betty was just no use. She had her family to look after.'

Friends and neighbours were more likely to be asked for supportive help than for challenging help, and these requests were usually met by friends but less frequently by neighbours.

Of the more formal groups, the medical profession rarely received challenging requests, whereas social services, housing departments and the police were often asked for such assistance. Obviously, statutory agencies have the resources and/or the sanctions that would be expected to provide meaningful challenges to the man's violence, while general practitioners do not:

> 'I used to go and talk to the doctor but there was nothing really she could do to help me. I mean it was outwith her

stand to do any more than she did apart from see the social work department and that's all they can do.'

'The doctor was helpful but there was nothing he could really do. He would just give you pills for your nerves and tell you it was up to you to sort things out.'

As these two accounts indicate, the responses of general practitioners were rather restricted. They rarely acted in a challenging way. Instead, responses were usually confined to treating wounds, prescribing psychotropic medications and sometimes referring women to psychiatrists. Women told us that they initially appreciated the medication, but some eventually realised that it provided no solutions and might even exacerbate their predicament.

'He put me on a course of tablets and I'd take the tablets and then would go back to see how the tablets helped and I'd tell him they did and I was fine. You weren't really telling lies because the tablets did help me but the same thing was happening again. I mean he was still hitting me. The tablets sort of calmed me down but they really didn't do much good.'

'I went to my doctor a lot but all he would ever give me was pills for my nerves but they were no use.'

One of the most insensitive and unhelpful forms of response came from a few general practitioners who set explicit criteria that women must meet before they were prepared to offer additional assistance.

'I used to go round to the doctor's quite often because I couldn't sleep at night and my nerves were bothering me and I wasn't eating, but he just said, "I can't help you while you're living with him; if he leaves or you leave him, come back and then maybe I'll be able to help you." '

'The doctor put me on drugs. He told me to get away and he asked me if I liked getting beaten up and I said "No!!" and he said "Well there must be something wrong with you because nobody could stand that much pain." '

Such responses can be seen against a background of adherence to negative views about women who experience violence. Research reveals that some medical practitioners think the problem is trivial or that battered women are bad housewives, hysterical, masochistic, or actually like the violence (Cartwright, 1967; Rounsaville, 1977; Rounsaville and Weissman, 1977-8; Hilberman and Munson, 1978; Stark, Flitcraft and Frazier, 1979; Pahl, 1979b; Binney, Harkell and Nixon, 1981). Such responses demonstrate a considerable failure to comprehend the predicament of battered women. Fortunately, not all general practitioners responded in these ways; some offered support and a few even attempted to challenge the husband with his culpability.

The referral to and contact with a psychiatrist is likely to entail implicit, sometimes explicit notions that the 'problem' probably resides in the woman's personality and/or behaviour. The long-standing psychiatric theories and professional ideologies that emphasize the provoking, masochistic and violence-seeking nature of women often result in victim blaming (Snell, Rosenwald and Robey, 1964; Storr, 1974; Gayford, 1976; Shainess, 1977; Bowder, 1979; Pizzey and Shapiro, 1982). The widespread, general views that women are responsible for the cause and solution of this and other problems in the family may exacerbate the woman's predicament and reinforce her sense of guilt while at the same time reinforcing the man's sense of justification.

'For a while I kept going to the psychiatrist thinking that
it was my fault and asking him to tell me what I was
doing wrong. He never really told me that it was my fault
but then again he never said it wasn't my fault.'

The social and psychological predicaments of battered women are mainly invisible to the medical profession. They escape the medical gaze almost entirely, and this is especially the case in the casualty ward (Rounsaville and Weissman, 1977-8; Stark, Flitcraft and Frazier, 1979; Women's Aid Federation (England), 1980b). The one-way hierarchical nature of the medical examination which excludes dialogue makes it very unlikely that women will raise the problem, and general practitioners are not likely to do so either. The doctor's failure to comprehend, or to seek to understand the problem must be understood relative to a background of patriarchal assumptions about women, institutional and situational demands made on the medical profession (too many patients, inadequate resources) and professional training that seeks to fit complex social, psychological and physical problems into neat, clear-cut physical symptoms that can be defined as treatable.

Social workers were usually asked for both supportive and challenging assistance. The most likely challenging requests were for tangible assistance such as accommodation or resources that would enable the woman to leave her husband.[8] Given this, women had greater expectations of social workers than of general practitioners. Yet, as far as responses are concerned, it was the supportive requests that were much more likely to be met than the challenging ones. One response that could be either supportive or challenging was casework counselling. However, this rarely included the man and could even have a negative effect if it resulted in blame being directed at the woman.

> 'I felt everybody was up against me, even socially. I felt inadequate as a woman. He was all right, he could do what he liked to me but nobody ever tried to help me. It seemed to me that the social workers and the doctors were blaming me for it.'

> 'The social workers were sympathetic but it was always a case of, if he did that to me, I'd have done this to him and I'd have done that to him. So it was my fault, and I think they believed him.'

There may be several reasons why social workers do not contact men and confront them about the violence. To the extent that the problem is seen primarily as the woman's this perception precludes the need to make contact with the man and also leads more easily to focusing upon the woman as the source of the trouble. In addition, many social workers, especially women, may be intimidated by the idea of confronting a man known to be violent to women. Although some social workers did attempt to confront the man and/or actively pursue assistance for the woman, they acted primarily upon individual initiative and not because of priorities or policies set by the agency.

The response of social workers generally reflected several concerns of fundamental importance to their profession: the protection and/or care of children, the maintenance of the family unit and the ideal of domestic privacy. The irony here is that the mere suspicion of child abuse almost always results in swift action and intervention that takes precedence over concern for family unity and domestic privacy while the certain knowledge of wife abuse rarely does so (Wilson, 1975; 1977; Dahl and Snare, 1978; Donzelot, 1980; Cavanagh,1981). Many of the women we interviewed gave accounts of how their requests and need for assistance were relegated to a secondary position or ignored (see also Service Delivery Assessment, 1980).

> 'I went to the welfare to get somewhere to stay but they couldn't help me. Mrs Jones [social worker] told me I would have to stay and I said, "I just can't," and they said, "You'll just have to stay for the sake of the wee ones." And at that stage I thought, "My God all anybody can ever say to me is the wee ones, the wee ones, but what about me?" '

> Once he [social worker] had made sure that the kids were in no danger he just went off and left me. And I thought, Huh, it seems nobody cares if I get beaten black and blue but if the kids do – which they weren't – then they get the attention I don't seem to deserve.

The salience of these concerns for children and maintenance of the family unit have been corroborated in the research of Maynard (this volume), who examined case notes of social workers dealing with women subjected to systematic violence. Her research revealed a general failure to focus on the violence directed at the woman along with an almost exclusive preoccupation with the welfare of children, the domestic skills of women and their supposed contribution to the violence. Furthermore, she found that while social workers apparently found it rather difficult to accept women's accounts of the violence, on the rare occasions when men were interviewed, their rationalisations and condemnations appeared to have been given more credence. As one of the

161

women we interviewed put it, 'Everybody seemed to think I was exaggerating every time I said anything about him.' In our study, social workers often advised women to simply cope with the violence and/or change their behaviour in order to appease their husband. The following are typical responses suggesting that women try to cope:

> (Q. 'Did the social worker ever give you any advice?')
> 'Patch it up. I thought I was going crackers with patch it up, patch it up, patch it up. . . . The Welfare all said to me . . . : "You've just got to stay in the home for the sake of the children. You've just got to keep the home together." And of course there was little else I could do because they wouldn't help me to get a house or anything.
> 'Just the usual, you know, just try and talk it over, try and patch it up.'

> (Q. And did you follow that advice?)
> 'I had to, there was nothing else I could do.'

Such negative or unhelpful responses to battered women reflect several factors: statutory obligations to protect children but not women, numerous professional ideals about family unity and domestic privacy, psychoanalytic views of women, traditional orientations towards the relationships between men and women and the concept of remaining 'neutral' (Nichols, 1976; Wilson, 1977; Pfouts, 1978; Schecter, 1978; Maynard, this volume). Regardless of the background to unhelpful, condemning or 'neutral' responses, the outcome often reinforces the man's domination and the woman's isolation and sense of guilt and shame, and, thus, reduces the probability that continued assistance will be sought. Among the women we interviewed, negative or unhelpful responses were the main reasons given for not seeking further assistance from physicians, social workers and the police.[9]

In order to overcome these problems and respond in a more effective manner, practitioners need to scrutinise their beliefs, actions and policies in order to eliminate those that support the violence. They need to respond in a clearer and more straightforward manner, adopting the role of the advocate in providing positive emotional support and material assistance for the woman while posing a direct challenge to male domination and violence. Statutory agencies must begin to confront the man with his own culpability, try to alter his sense of rightful control and condemn his use of violence as a means of settling disputes with his wife. This, of course, is not an easy task and will require development of training programmes, referral systems and back-up networks. The involvement of both formal agencies and feminist community groups such as Women's Aid, which have served as a model for responding in a direct and positive fashion to the victims of violence, is essential in all these developments.

Our findings indicate that the timing of responses may be important. In the beginning of a violent relationship, some men express shame, guilt and remorse about their violent actions. This would seem to be an excellent point to begin to work on alternative conceptions and reactions. Although the initial ambivalence of women about seeking assistance may make this difficult in some cases, those who do come forward at an early stage should be responded to positively and immediately rather than put off with a 'wait and see' response.

These findings demonstrate that battered women suffer from severe and persistent violence, that they are hemmed in by social, moral and material forces, that help seeking is a complex and multi-layered process not necessarily related directly to the severity of a particular violent assault, and that the nature of agency responses plays a direct role in this overall process. Evidence such as this challenges speculations that battered women suffer from 'learned helplessness', are 'violence-seeking' or 'violence-prone'. On the contrary, women who are abused engage in an active struggle to find solutions to the violence and to seek the help of outsiders in these efforts.

Notes

1   This research was partially supported by the Scottish Home and Health Department, and the final draft of this paper was completed while the authors were scholars in residence at the Rockefeller Foundation Study and Conference Center, Bellagio, Lake Como, Italy.

2 The research programme from which this paper arises is based on a generally reflexive and context-specific methodology and involved a number of interrelated empirical strategies including historical analysis, in-depth interviews with 109 battered women and the examination of 34,000 police and court records. The context-dependent technique used in the systematic in-depth interviews allowed the women to discuss the violence and their reactions to it relative to their own experiences and backgrounds, rather than to a series of abstract questions. This technique allowed us to collect detailed descriptions of the problem and the relationships in which it occurred as well as information about meanings and interpretations associated with the problem and relationships.

These interviews usually lasted two and a half hours, although a few extended beyond ten hours and they were all tape recorded and transcribed in order to retain the qualitative materials. The women interviewed ranged in age from 18 to 60, the majority were under the age of 30. Over 85 per cent were married to the man who used violence against them and the majority came from urban, working-class families. Most of the interviews, ninety-three, were conducted in Women's Aid refuges and the remainder were carried out in the homes of the women (Dobash and Dobash, 1979; 1983).

3 Collectively, the 109 women reported receiving approximately 32,000 assaults throughout their married lives.

4 Other researchers have explored the relationship between the severity of violence and factors such as leaving, divorcing, intervention, and duration of the relationship (Gelles, 1979; Pagelow,1981). While some interesting findings have emerged from this work, the use of survey techniques has resulted in a somewhat restricted and unidimensional measurement of severity of violence (e.g. using only the form of attack, Gelles, 1979, p. 99) and severely limited the collection of information about the dynamic aspects of the problem. By contrast, the systematic, in-depth method employed in this research allowed for the collection of extensive qualitative and quantitative data about specific violent attacks, their dynamic development and the wider context in which they occurred.

5 For a variety of technical reasons, thirteen of the 327 violent events could not be included in the analysis.

6 The three specific violent events, *first, worst,* and *last* were examined in order to consider three time periods in the relationship as well as the extreme point of violence. The *typical* assault was studied in order to provide information about the majority of violent events experienced by the women. In order to do this, a large number of detailed and identical questions were asked about each event. It should be noted that while the responses to those about the specific episodes are descriptions of the event, those about the typical assault were, of necessity, characterisations of the event.

7 Although exceedingly time-consuming, this was done in order to combat the problem of becoming overly abstract and of developing categories that either fail to represent the basic information in the verbatim accounts or misconstrue it. For a critical evaluation of abstract scales and a fuller discussion of the context-specific method employed in this research see Dobash and Dobash (1979; 1983).

8 It is important to note that even though requests concerning accommodation may be made to social work departments, these resources are the remit of housing departments. For a study of the housing needs of battered women see Women's Aid Federation (England) (1981).

9 For research on police and judicial responses to wife beating see Berk and Loseke (1981); Dobash and Dobash (1981b); Wasoff (1982).

Chapter eleven

Refuges and housing for battered women

Val Binney, Gina Harkell and
Judy Nixon

One of the questions so often asked in any discussion of battering is, 'Why do women stay and put up with it?' What is usually overlooked is the extent to which women have been trapped in violent relationships simply because they have had nowhere else to go. The opening of refuges in the early 1970s did much to publicise the existence of violent husbands and the need of women to escape from them. In 1977 the Department of Environment commissioned the Women's Aid Federation to undertake a national survey of refuges and housing for battered women in England and Wales, to examine the extent of refuge provision which had become available and what sort of service it was offering, and to examine the effectiveness of two recent pieces of legislation – the Housing (Homeless Persons) Act, 1977 and the Domestic Violence Act, 1976. This chapter is based on that survey (Binney, Harkell and Nixon, 1981).

The survey took place in 1978 and a total of 114 refuges out of the 150 traced returned questionnaires on the organisation of their refuge; 656 women living in 128 refuges were interviewed. In the light of these findings we can discuss women's need for emergency accommodation, the role of refuges in meeting these needs and, finally, the problems women encountered in finding a permanent home. Our findings challenge the idea that battered women are not serious about leaving violent men. They also show that finding any sort of accommodation, let alone accommodation which meets their needs, makes leaving home a gruelling experience for most women. That so many women finally made a separate home for themselves attests more to their strength and determination than to the co-operation of the statutory agencies involved.

Women's need for refuge

The study showed that refuges are providing accommodation for a very large number of families each year. The 150 refuges traced had accommodated an estimated 11,400 women and 20,850 children between September 1977 and September 1978, and had turned away many more. At any one time there were approximately 1,000 women and 1,700 children in refuges.

The vast majority of women had left home to escape physical violence to themselves and sometimes (in 27 per cent of cases) also to their children. Assaults ranged from kicks and punches to attempted strangulation, suffocation and drowning. Mental cruelty had taken the form of verbal taunting and reducing women to a state where they doubted their own sanity. The average length of time women had suffered violence was seven years and ranged from a few months to thirty or forty years. As violence had usually started when women were in their early twenties, it was generally the case that the older a woman was, the longer she had suffered. The average age of women in refuges was 31, but ranged from 17 to 70.

Most women had wanted to leave their violent partner from within the first year of marriage but their main obstacle had been that they had nowhere to go. Most had only recently heard of the existence of refuges, but had managed to leave home before, three times on average, usually staying with relatives or friends. However, this usually offered only a temporary breathing space to women, rather than the opportunity to make a permanent break. There was seldom enough room for a woman to stay with her children for long and she was easily found by her husband or boyfriend. The importance of keeping her whereabouts secret was clear from the pressures that came into play once a woman was found. Although some women had genuinely sought a reconciliation, all too often women described being simply worn down by their husband's persuasions to return. A proportion had been literally forced back – physically or because of threats – while others did not want to impose their husband's behaviour on their friends or relatives:

> 'I went to my parents and of course, he came – I left him because of his hitting and kicking me – and I went home to them, but he came there and I had to go. I went back really to keep the peace because my parents weren't able to cope with it.'

Finding temporary accommodation was even more difficult if women had no friends or relatives on hand to turn to. A third of women had never stayed with relatives in the past and 14 per cent had been entirely dependent on formal sources of accommodation. Some women described spending nights in telephone boxes and public lavatories after violent attacks; others had left home not knowing where they would end up that night. The desperation and uncertainty of leaving home are expressed here by Stella:

> 'I ran out the back door and all I had on was my knickers and bra, but he'd kicked me so bad, I couldn't go back. So I managed to pull an overall off the line. I ran in such a panic, and I ran and I ran along the main road, and this car stopped and I asked where they were going. It was Carlisle so I said, "Can I go there too?" With it being dark, they didn't realise the state I was in, so I got to Carlisle and was dropped off and just sat there on a park bench. I didn't know where I was, I had no money, I had no coat. It was absolutely freezing, I had no shoes and no socks, I had nothing on at all and I sat there for about four or five hours. The daylight was come and people were passing me and they must have thought I was mental or something. But I was in such agony and such pain I just wanted the ground to open up and die. In the end I managed to get to the police station and they took me to a battered women's home.'

Agency response to battered women

Despite increasing recognition of violence against women in the home, agencies were frequently failing to give battered women the help they asked for. On average women had approached five separate agencies for help in the past. However, half of all consultations were regarded as unhelpful. What is worse is that the agencies most able to meet women's needs for protection and accommodation, that is the police and housing departments, were found to be least helpful by women. Only a third of women consulting either of these agencies found the contact of any value. Housing departments frequently told women that there was nothing that could be done: 'They couldn't do anything about rehousing me while he was in the house.' 'I told them about my husband breaking up the house and they just said I'd have to pay for it.' Women had not only been discouraged from seeking long-term alternative accommodation. Housing departments had also only referred 8 per cent of women to refuges. They tended instead to put women in bed and breakfast accommodation, hostels or homeless families' units where they gained little help in reorganising their lives or arranging a permanent home away from the violent man.

In seeking help from agencies, women often complained that the violence itself became the focus of attention rather than their desire to leave home, ironically making it harder for a woman suffering violence to separate than anyone else. The emphasis of most agencies was on reconciliation rather than on providing escape routes, their argument being that women usually go back to their husbands anyway. Our study disproves this assumption. Only 16 per cent of women traced a year after the original survey had returned to their husbands or boyfriends.

The growth of refuges

By 1978 when the survey took place, refuge provision in England and Wales had reached only one-sixth of the level recommended by the Select Committee on Violence in Marriage in 1975. Some areas had no refuges at all while even large metropolitan areas such as the West Midlands had only 6 per cent of the estimated number needed. The main obstacle to increased refuge provision was the unwillingness of local authorities to support such projects. Groups of women had usually had to campaign for over a year to get properties from the council, while some had been campaigning for four to five years and still had not succeeded. In September 1978 at least thirty groups were still trying to get a property to use as a refuge and four years later the number remained the same. This was despite the fact that under the Housing (Homeless Persons) Act, housing departments have a duty to house battered women and so it is not in their interest to discourage local women's groups from supplying it at little or no cost to themselves.

Not only have local councils discouraged the setting up of refuges, but they have also frequently provided women's aid groups with poor quality housing for use as refuges. The vast majority of refuges were rented from the council – 83 per cent in 1978. Yet in the period between 1974 and 1978, 202 houses had been opened as refuges and a quarter had been closed. They had usually had to be demolished or closed on health grounds. Generally the condition of refuges was well below that of average family accommodation and they were often in areas about to be redeveloped.

'The house is a small two-bedroomed terraced house with a downstairs room used as an extra bedroom. The rooms are dark and dingy. We have constant electrical faults. The house is the only one on the street that is lived in as it is a demolition area. It has been broken into several times and things stolen and twice the phone has been ripped off the wall. There is no play space so kids use the street which is littered with broken glass.'

Half the groups complained about poor maintenance of property by their council landlords and nearly all councils charged the refuge group full council rent – on average £16 a week – for each house.

The poor condition of property was exacerbated by the large numbers of women and children. Most refuges were severely overcrowded at the time of the survey and no decrease in numbers has been reported since. There were on average six women and nine children per refuge – usually three-bedroomed. Nearly half the women had to share bedrooms with other families, while almost all shared with their own children, whatever their age and sex. Women frequently slept in bunk beds with their children and occasionally on the settee when overcrowding was at its height. There was usually one kitchen and cooker, one bathroom and no dining room or laundry room. For those who have not been to a refuge, the extent of overcrowding is difficult to imagine. But if you can imagine your own family multiplied by five all living in a rundown house with only one cooker, and imagine the washing of about fifteen people hung around the one gas fire in the living room, and a lot of noisy children running around with nothing to do because there is no playroom and no toys, then you might get an idea of what it is like to live in a refuge.

Some women's aid groups had managed to obtain good refuge accommodation, either purpose built or converted, usually from housing associations. Generally it seemed that refuges worked best when houses were not too large or shared by too many people – five or six families seemed the maximum. The sort of accommodation that would suit the majority of women in our survey would consist of a separate bedroom, a kitchen and bathroom shared with only one or two other families and communal living room and playroom.

Living in a refuge

Despite the appalling conditions and overcrowding in many refuges, the women we interviewed talked very positively about their experience of living there. For the first time, women had safe accommodation for as long as they needed it, together with practical help and advice on how to organise a permanent separation. The institutionalisation often experienced in hostels was avoided in most refuges as residents usually organised day-to-day running of the place themselves. Generally women said they had gained from the experience and volunteered far more features of refuge life that they liked than that they disliked. Sixty-five per cent of women said their mental health had improved:

'I'm going back to how I used to be – happy and carefree.
It's been the change of me, the change of the children.
My health's got better, so has theirs. I can control them
now. I couldn't before. They saw him hit me so they did
too.'

Women found it a great relief to be able to talk to other
women about their experiences: 'I used to be ashamed to talk
about battering to people. I can really talk openly here because
they've all been through the same thing.'

Women also said that their children's physical and mental
health had often improved since being in the refuge. Problems
such as bedwetting, and illnesses made worse by stress, such
as asthma, had declined.

Although women and children had benefited from coming
to a refuge, the conditions were totally unsuitable for long-
term stays. After a few months women often despaired of ever
finding somewhere permanent to live. Most women felt that a
stay of two months was ideal, with six months the absolute
maximum. However, because of the difficulty of finding
permanent accommodation, women were having to stay on
average five and a half months, with 30 per cent staying longer
than that – in many cases over a year.

Despite the difficulties of refuge life, over half the women
interviewed preferred having come through a refuge than to
have been rehoused immediately. Eighteen months later when
we interviewed eighty-four women in the second stage of the
research, this figure had jumped to 83 per cent, often because
of continuing contact with the refuge and friends made while
they were living there. However, a minority of women felt
they had not benefited from being in a refuge and some other
form of help would be more appropriate for these women.

Refuges are the only accommodation available to battered
women in this country which deal specifically with their
needs. They are also assisting government agencies to fulfil
their duties to the homeless. Despite this saving in cost, refuge
groups generally received little financial assistance from
housing authorities. Only 10 per cent of groups received
money from local housing departments in 1978 and the
average amount was £785.

The chief sources of funding for refuges were rent from

residents and, in some cases, grant funding for paid workers. In 1978, two-thirds of groups received such a grant either from the Manpower Services Commission or from Urban Aid. The former has since virtually disappeared as a source of funding for refuges and Urban Aid is limited to cerain areas. Refuges have now been running for over a decade and they have demonstrated their importance to battered women and their children. Local authorities should recognise that the experimental phase for refuges is now over and should offer them funding as part of their main programme. Even when adequately funded, refuges still provide a much cheaper and more suitable form of accommodation than hostels, bed and breakfast accommodation or homeless families' units, as they are predominantly run by the women living in them rather than by paid supervisors.

Finding permanent housing

So far we have looked at the need for emergency accommodation for battered women and the extent to which current provision is inadequate. Turning to the question of permanent housing, we find once again that women experienced many obstacles trying to obtain it, despite recent legislation aimed at making the process easier.

The vast majority of women (81 per cent) were trying to obtain permanent housing from local authorities, while 31 per cent were trying to return to their previous home with the violent man legally excluded. Other options being pursued were trying to find private rented flats or houses, or applying to a housing association. Half the women were trying more than one of these routes at the same time. However, on leaving refuges only 63 per cent of women went into some form of permanent housing and only 44 per cent into council housing. Contrary to popular belief, women returning to violent partners from the refuge made up only 14 per cent of the total. A much greater cause for concern were the 15 per cent of women still in emergency forms of accommodation a year after their original interview. A mere 8 per cent of women returned to their former homes after having their husband or boyfriend excluded.

Thus, neither of the two most popular routes to rehousing – that is, the local authority and excluding the man from the former home – had proved very successful. The impact of the Housing (Homeless Persons) Act of 1977 and the Domestic Violence Act, 1976 are discussed below, in the light of these women's experiences and those of groups running refuges.

The Housing (Homeless Persons) Act imposed duties on local authorites to house women made homeless by domestic violence or threat of violence. However, sections of the Act are open to differing interpretations, which have given rise to considerable differences in practice across the country. At the time of the first interview, local authorities had rejected 207 applications (43 per cent) to be rehoused as a homeless person. An examination of the grounds on which women were turned down reveals the extent to which the act was being ignored in some cases and very narrowly interpreted in others.

Deciding that women were 'not homeless' was the most common reason given for refusal to rehouse. Some women were told they were not battered because they could not show visible bruising or produce other evidence of assault. Others were given no reason at all. In some cases it was argued that although women were battered, they were living in a refuge and therefore were not homeless. Another reason given for refusal was that women had come to a refuge from another area and were therefore the responsibility of the previous local authority. Contrary to the act, these women were being sent back to areas where they were in danger of further violence. Some women and children were shunted back and forth between two authorities, with neither prepared to accept responsibility for them. Other women had been told they were 'not in priority need', this reason being given particularly to women without dependent children. The Code of Guidance accompanying the Act expressly stated the need for battered women without children to be eligible for rehousing, but as it is left to the discretion of local authorities rather than being a duty, many councils were refusing to assist such women. Pregnant women had also been refused, contrary to the terms of the Act itself. Some women had been refused because they had become 'homeless intentionally', all manner of vague reasons being given. Fifty women were put on the ordinary waiting list and expected to have to wait several years to be rehoused. In such cases no reference to the Act had been made at all.

Once accepted by local authorities for rehousing, women had further obstacles to overcome. Many were told to fulfil certain conditions, such as obtaining a divorce or custody of the children, which could be lengthy procedures. Rent arrears on the former home had frequently been built up during or since the time women had left home. Paying off such arrears was usually made a condition of rehousing and women had to do so out of meagre social security payments. The Department of Health and Social Security is empowered to pay two rents simultaneously under special circumstances, but few women's aid groups had been able to secure this concession for women in their refuges.

Thus the process of being rehoused by local authorities was often a long and complicated one, despite the homelessness legislation. Women had made better progress and were more satisfied when they had approached the local authority where the refuge was based, regardless of whether they came from that area originally. It seems that having a Women's Aid group on the spot to back up applications was more important than a previous connection with the area. Some groups had developed a good relationship with the local housing department over the years and developed a co-operative approach to the smooth rehousing of women from their refuge. Others felt this was impossible with their particular authority and acted as 'watchdogs', putting pressure on the authority to fulfil its obligations under the Housing (Homeless Persons) Act.

It has been argued that the Housing (Homeless Persons) Act has improved the housing prospects of battered women. However, evidence from our own survey and other sources suggests that this is not so. Less than half the Women's Aid groups thought that the housing prospects of women in their refuge had improved since the Act. Some groups said it had become more difficult to get women rehoused because authorities had tightened up their criteria in order to limit their responsibilities under the Act. Eighteen months later, many groups felt that the gains of the Act were only temporary and had been eroded later as a result of local authority spending cuts. For example, the average length of time women had to wait in some refuges for local authority housing had increased from six months to a year. This was particularly true of London.

An examination of local authorities' homelessness returns to the Department of Environment for 1978 also revealed that battered women, once accepted as homeless, were receiving different treatment from other homeless groups. Fewer battered women were rehoused immediately and, excluding those referred to a refuge or hostel, more were put into bed and breakfast accommodation (Department of the Environment, 1978). A GLC Research Memorandum shares this view:

> 'Some authorities are taking a comparatively hard line towards these people . . . making every effort to try and induce them to return to their former homes and advocating the use of the rather limited remedies contained in the 1976 *Domestic Violence Act*.' (Kenny and Thompson, 1978)

Returning to the former home – the Domestic Violence Act, 1976

The Domestic Violence Act was intended to make a woman's home safe for her to live in, by excluding the violent partner with a court injunction. Our study highlights two drawbacks in practice. Firstly, it was not so easy to get an exclusion order; the violence has to be proved to be severe before judges will consider throwing a man out of the joint home, and even more severe and persistent for police powers of arrest to be attached to the injunction. The second major drawback was the difficulty of getting the injunction enforced. In our follow-up study, seventeen of the eighty-four women had called the police because of their husband's violence since obtaining an injunction. However only four men out of the seventeen committing assault were charged with breaking the injunction, although ten of the women had suffered life-threatening attacks or an injury which required hospitalisation. Even when the man had been found guilty, the punishment was light. Fines ranged from £20 to £75 and none of the men were imprisoned. Response by the police to women with injunctions was again placatory. They would try and smooth things over and then go away again. Women were told that their husbands could not be arrested without a powers of arrest clause to their injunction, but even if they had one, our study shows that the police were no more likely to arrest the man. As one woman said:

'He punched me about, I had a knife to my throat, just generally what he does. I called the police but they didn't arrest him. I asked them to take him back to Derby but they didn't. They offered him a cup of tea and then put him in the garden and he was there all night throwing stones and shouting. And my face was out here (with bruising).' (Woman rehoused in Nottingham with non-molestation order and exclusion order with powers of arrest)

In September 1978, thirty-two women who had obtained exclusion orders were still living in a refuge, either because they were too afraid to move back home or because the man refused to move out. Generally this route to rehousing was the least successful. Out of 411 women from the original survey, only 8 per cent finally left the refuge to return to their previous home and only 4 per cent were still living there a year later.

The quality of housing women obtained

Eighteen months after the first interview, the majority of women in permanent accommodation were in council housing (83 per cent) while 12 per cent were in housing association property. The latter was usually of higher quality. Nearly half the women in council property described their housing as poor, but most had felt obliged to accept whatever they were offered in case no other offers were made. Seventy per cent of properties were said to have needed repairs doing to them when women moved in. It had taken an average of five months to have this work done, while some women were still waiting after eighteen months.

The areas where women had been rehoused varied considerably from rural 1930s council estates to rundown 'problem family' areas or half-boarded-up development zones.

The most frequent complaints were that there was nowhere for the children to play and that the area was 'rough'. Also single mothers often felt they were an easy target for harassment from gangs of teenage boys as there was no man around 'to put an end to all that nonsense'.

Usually women had had no choice about where they were rehoused and often found themselves isolated miles from family and friends. Although a third of women would have liked a joint tenancy with another friend, often from the refuge, both for company and for help with their children, no one in this survey had obtained one.

Conclusion

Without access to alternative accommodation it is exceedingly difficult for women to leave violent men. Our study showed that the specific sorts of help and accommodation offered by refuges had made it possible for many battered women to make a permanent break. However, refuges were only the first stage in the long and arduous business of leaving home. Finding permanent housing is not easy despite the Housing (Homeless Persons) Act and the Domestic Violence Act, both of which should have increased women's chances. Tightening of criteria by local authorities in the face of their new responsibilities and the effects of spending cuts have eroded many of the gains won by recent legislation.

Little has so far been done to provide housing which meets the specific needs of battered women and their children. After long periods of violence and insecurity, women needed a decent standard of safe accommodation in areas which did not isolate them from family and friends and where they would not be harassed. Our study shows that rather than being treated sympathetically, they were more likely to be sent to the bottom of the pile.

PART III

Conclusion

Jan Pahl

Chapter twelve

Implications for policy and practice

This final chapter returns to the scene with which the book began, that is to the conference on Violence in the Family at which all the papers in Part II of this book were presented. The conference was designed so that the presentation of research findings was followed by discussion group sessions in which all participants were able to contribute from their own experience to a discussion of the problems thrown up by the research. The participants included social workers and health service workers, members of the police and of the legal profession, workers from a number of Women's Aid refuges, representatives of Women's Aid from England, Scotland, Ireland and Wales, housing managers, policy makers from a number of government departments, and representatives of a wide range of voluntary organisations. Each discussion group contained a broad spectrum of expertise and at the end of the seminar the groups made written recommendations which reflected their discussions over the previous three days. This chapter draws on the reports of the discussion groups and on the findings of the research, to make recommendations for future policy and practice in the field of wife abuse. Finally, the chapter returns to the more general theoretical issue of the ways in which conceptions of privacy can militate against both short-term and long-term solutions to wife abuse.

Any recommendations for policy changes will inevitably be greeted with scepticism. Proposals for minor changes are likely to be accused of alleviating the effects of a problem while leaving its fundamental structural causes unaltered; proposals for fundamental changes are likely to be discarded as impractical or dangerous. Yet an issue such as wife abuse, which presents an immediate problem to a wide range of professionals, while also raising fundamental questions about the nature of gender relationships, is likely to give rise to a list of 'policy recommendations' which seeks for change at a number of different levels. (See Hanmer and Leonard, 1984.)

Firstly, it is important to recognise that housing is a central issue. Both in the short term and in the long term, abused women need safe accommodation, so that they are not forced to go on living with a violent man, and so that it becomes possible for them to make a new life for themselves and their children. There are a variety of ways in which the long-term, housing needs of battered women may be met. It should be possible for women living in local authority housing to remain in their own homes if they so wish and to have the tenancy transferred to them without having to take responsibility for their ex-husband's rent arrears. Alternatively, if women do not feel safe in their own home area it should be possible for them to be transferred to another local authority even if their husband has run up rent arrears in their home area. At present the short-term housing needs of battered women are met either through refuges or through the provision of temporary accommodation by local authorities, from which women are eventually rehoused in permanent accommodation. It is important that there be more effective monitoring of the ways in which local authorities are carrying out their duties under the Housing (Homeless Persons) Act. At present there is evidence that many local authorities are evading their responsibilities, for example, by defining abused women as voluntarily homeless, or by sending women back to their home area despite their fear of further assault. Battered women without children, like other single homeless women, are in a particularly difficult position, since they are not defined as being in priority need under the Housing (Homeless Persons) Act. They form one of the most disadvantaged sections of the population as far as housing is concerned, so it is important that refuges continue to offer them shelter.

Secondly, it is crucial to recognise the importance of Women's Aid, at present the primary agency for helping battered women. A number of studies have documented the value of refuges in offering women practical help, a roof over their heads for as long as they need it and protection from further assault, while fostering mutual support among the women in a way that does seem to enhance confidence and self-esteem. Yet the total number of refuges still does not come near to the recommendation of the Select Committee on Violence in Marriage that there should be one refuge place per 10,000 of the population. Not only are there not enough refuges, but most of those that exist are desperately under-funded. This bears harshly on the women and children who stay there, in terms of overcrowding and poor facilities, and it places a severe burden on those who are trying to set up or run a refuge. Most refuges are run by voluntary groups who employ paid workers if they can afford to do so; few have any long-term financial security. Work in refuges is stressful and demanding and those who work there are paid modestly, if at all, so it is hardly surprising that there are not nearly enough refuges and that those which exist teeter permanently on the brink of closure. The most common source of funding is the local authority, partly, no doubt, because refuges provide a cheap way for councils to fulfil their responsibilities (Barr and Carrier, 1978). The Manpower Services Commission is an important source of funding for paid workers. However, this is essentially a short-term source of funds. It is vital that a secure, long-term source of funding be found for Women's Aid refuges.

A major difficulty in identifying a source of funding for refuges is that the problem of any one woman may be the responsibility of a number of different agencies. The Housing Department, the Social Services Department, the Health Service, the Social Security, the police and the law may each have something to offer – but each can all too easily refer the woman on. Referring can be the most appropriate course of action, or it can be a way of escaping responsibility. Battered women, like other unpopular client groups, are low on priority lists, not least because of the fact that the more agencies are involved in the care of any one client group, the lower will that client group stand in the list of priorities of any one agency. It is important that central government makes it clear where responsibility lies for providing funding for Women's Aid. One suggestion has come from the Convention of Scottish Local Authorities. This recommends funding local groups working on behalf of battered women on the basis of 50 per cent from Central Government, 25 per cent from Housing Authorities and 25 per cent from Social Services Departments (Convention of Scottish Local Authorities, 1980). A variant of this suggestion would be the recommendation that providing housing for refuge groups should be the responsibility of the Housing Department, providing funding for paid workers should be the responsibility of the Social Services Department, while the responsibility for running refuges should remain with Women's Aid groups.

Thirdly, there is an urgent need for training for all those professionals who meet abused women in the course of their work. Better practice and greater understanding need not cost money but they do require determination and action. It is particularly important that those who are in a position to help battered women are knowledgeable about the relevant legislation, about women's rights to social security benefits and housing, and about the whereabouts of the nearest women's refuge. The topic of wife abuse should be covered both in the basic training and in the in-service training of all the relevant professions. In-service training could take the form of day workshops, such as those organised by the Canterbury Social Services Department, or longer residential courses, such as those run by the Scottish Health Education Group. These courses could be backed by teaching packages, such as those pioneered by the University of Dundee and now being prepared by the Open University.

Many professionals feel isolated and inadequate when faced with an abused women. This is a product not just of their own lack of knowledge, but also of the lack of understanding of the issue among higher levels of management. Too often the efforts of grass-roots workers are undermined by the prejudiced attitudes and lack of interest shown by their superiors. Too often the comment is made that there is no point in helping a woman because she will only return to her husband, without any understanding of the broader context and of the pressures exerted on women to return; the scepticism of professionals must be counted among the pressures forcing women back into violent relationships. The tendency of women to return to their husbands can discourage the most enlightened professional. It is important to remember that the

184

research reported in this book concluded that women who go to refuges are in general women whose marriages are ending. The breakdown of these marriages can be painful and protracted and those involved professionally should not desert a woman who returns temporarily to her husband. It has been suggested that local networks of communication should be established between agencies to provide a framework within which abused women can be supported and advised. This would be similar to the current arrangements for dealing with the non-accidental injury of children: it is striking how minimal is the concern for abused women compared with that for abused children.

Fourthly, there is the problem of the gap between legislation and implementation, between theory and practice. This shows itself in many different ways, but especially in the areas of housing and of policing. The exercise of discretion can result in the partial implementation of legislation, and this partial implementation is not random but tends to reflect and reinforce particular patterns of social relationships. Taking the example of the police, Faragher has shown how the gap between theory and practice has the effect of making assault on a wife less serious than assault on a stranger (Faragher, this volume). This in its turn diminishes public concern about the problem. It takes a conscious change of policy to alter the pattern.

Such a change was recently introduced by the Minneapolis Police Department. The change was the result of a controlled experiment in which police officers used three different tactics in response to cases of wife assault. The tactics were arrest, mediation, or ordering the violent spouse to leave for eight hours. The unique aspect of the study was that the police response was assigned to them at random before they arrived at the scene of the violence. According to police records, only 10 per cent of the men who were arrested went on to repeat the offence within six months, compared with 16 per cent of those who were given mediation or counselling, and 22 per cent of those ordered out of the house. Admitting that policemen had 'psychological barriers' to overcome in arresting men who abused their wives, the Minneapolis Chief of Police has now restructured police training and police practice in such a way that it will be difficult for offenders in domestic violence cases to avoid arrest (Sherman and Berk, 1984).

Fifthly, it is important to consider the children of violent fathers. What are the effects on them of the violence and of the experience of leaving home and going to a refuge? There has been considerable anxiety, both inside and outside of the refuge movement, about the effects of refuge life on children. Though many refuges make special provision by employing a child care worker or playgroup leader, older children some- times find refuge life difficult and some return to their fathers or go to stay with friends or relatives. This whole area is one in which there is a need for further research. It is important however, that a concern for the children does not diminish concern for the women; as Maynard has shown, an emphasis on children can obscure the different but equally valid interests of their mothers. (Maynard, this volume)

There is also a need for further research on the men themselves. To what extent is their violence a product of psychological factors, as opposed to being the product of social norms whch condone and support male violence. As we saw in chapter 1, male violence against women has a long history and is still given covert approval by some and casual acceptance by many. What are the sources of this casual acceptance and how may norms be changed? Could the level of domestic violence be reduced by giving boys the same sort of education for personal relationships and parenthood that girls now receive? All too often it is assumed that only girls need classes in preparation for marriage and family life, while in reality it may be more important to focus on boys. What sorts of responses are most effective in deterring men from renewed violence? Many agencies now work on the assump- tion that conciliation and mediation are appropriate, whereas it may be that treating wife assault as the crime it is would prove a more effective deterrent. We need more research both on the effectiveness of different ways of treating violent men, and on the fundamental question of challenging the norms and values which support male violence (Wilson, 1983).

Sixthly, work on wife abuse raises the question of the need to rethink the notion of 'the family'. There are still those who see the typical worker as a family man, with a wife who is not in employment, but who stays at home to care for their two children, without realising that such 'typical' workers represent a mere 5 per cent of the total labour force (Study Commission on the Family, 1983). With more than half of married women in paid employment, it is now the norm for both parents to work outside the home. With one in three marriages ending in divorce, the one-parent family can no longer be regarded as a deviant or temporary family form. With an unemployment rate approaching 14 per cent there are now many households where the woman is the chief earner. All these facts must lead to a questioning of the old assumptions about the nature of family life and about the allocation of money within the family. It is no longer possible to assume the financial dependence of the married woman, as, for example, in the payment of supplementary benefits to the man as 'head' of the household. A change to paying benefits to women in their own right would not only reflect reality more closely, but also ease the financial difficulties of many abused women (Homer, Leonard and Taylor, 1984).

'Family policy' reflects the confusion about what is meant by the family. On the one hand the family is seen as the institution responsible for the upbringing of children and the care of the sick, the handicapped and the elderly. Yet little support is given for the work done in the home, the invalid care allowance is denied to married women, and community care policies lay an increasing burden on women. On the other hand the employment of married women is recognised as a permanent phenomenon, keeping millions of children out of poverty. Yet little support is given to mothers who take employment; child care facilities are being cut back, women's wages for full time work are still only 70 per cent of men's wages, and a married woman whose pre-tax pay is the same as that of a married man will take less money home because she pays more tax than he does. The disadvantaged position of women is one element in prolonging wife abuse since it maintains the dependent position of wives and makes it more difficult for them to leave violent relationships (Barrett and McIntosh, 1982).

Finally, it is important to consider the fundamental structural roots of violence against wives. Wife abuse is not an isolated and rare event. As the contributors to this book have shown, it is the product of a complex and interrelated set of social phenomena of which the following are important

187

elements: the financial and legal dependence of married women; the assumption of male dominance within marriage; the reluctance of agencies to become involved in what is defined as a private matter; the emphasis, if they do become involved, on reconciliation, rather than on finding a long-term solution which protects the woman from further violence. For a fuller understanding of the problem we return to the issue of privacy, as it operates to insulate the family from society in a way that makes it possible for husbands to abuse their wives.

Whose privacy?

The question of the distinction between public and private has been raised by many of the contributors to this book. Part I documented the experiences of forty-two women as they attempted to find satisfactory alternatives to life with a violent husband. This study showed that one crucial element in the problem is that the violence is often ignored or minimised because it takes place within marriage and within the home, and that respect for the sanctity of marriage and for the privacy of the home can prevent women asking for, or getting, the help they need.

In Part II Parker pointed out that the reluctance of the law to intervene between a married couple, until the marriage breaks down and divorce is sought, reflects the ideology of privacy which is itself one cause of marital problems. Faragher discussed police intervention and, in answer to those who are concerned about police intervention into the private sphere and police erosion of individual liberties, asked the questions, 'Whose privacy? Whose liberty?' Maynard analysed the ways in which the privatised nature of family life and the dependent position of wives within families serves to maintain men's subordination of women on social, sexual and economic levels. Dobash, Dobash and Cavanagh showed how the battered woman's need for help changes over time, but that responses to this need are often inhibited by ideologies concerning domestic privacy and the wife's responsibility for the reputation and happiness of the couple's marriage. Binney, Harkell and Nixon demonstrated the centrality of housing to this issue and the ways in which housing constraints have the effect of trapping women and children in the privacy of violent homes.

In their study of responses to marital violence, Borkowski, Murch and Walker concluded that privacy was a central issue. This research team interviewed a wide range of practitioners and found that concern about the privacy of clients varied from one profession to another. Social workers and health visitors were much more concerned about invading privacy than were doctors and solicitors; on the other hand, solicitors and doctors were more likely to see themselves as bound by the principles of confidentiality in ways that they saw as protecting their clients' privacy. Borkowski, Murch and Walker suggested that respect for privacy represents respect for a couple's private life and for the distinctive identity of a couple's relationship. They pointed to the significance of 'boundary control' round a relationship. A husband exercises boundary control when he frightens his wife into keeping his violence a secret; a wife breaches the boundary when she discloses the violence to an outsider. The team concluded:

> We have found it helpful to think of two contradictory forces at work affecting the flow of information about marital violence – one seeking to keep it private, the other trying to make it public. In studying the response of community services to marital violence, one is to some extent studying the dynamic interaction between these forces, often operating simultaneously and creating ambiguities and dilemmas for the people concerned, clientele and practitioners alike. (Borkowski, Murch and Walker, 1983, 112)

Evidence from research into the circumstances of families involved in divorce proceedings suggests that people with marital problems do consider the question of privacy before deciding to which agency to go. Some people may hesitate for a long time before commencing divorce proceedings because they fear the public shame and stigmatisation they think will be involved. Such hesitations are particularly likely when violence is one of the causes given for the divorce; a woman may fear the anger of her spouse at her breach of the couple's privacy as well as being afraid of public reactions to the failure of the marriage. Similar considerations face women giving evidence in criminal prosecutions arising from marital violence (Elston, Fuller and Murch, 1975; Davis and Murch, 1977).

In a continuing discussion about the nature of privacy carried on over a number of years in the *Journal of Philosophy and Public Affairs*, the example of a husband and wife quarrelling was used to illustrate a point about the limits of the right to privacy. Thompson argued that if a passer-by happens to hear a couple quarrelling loudly their right to privacy is not thereby violated; on the other hand if the passer-by trains an amplifier on the house this constitutes an infringement of the right to privacy because the right not to be listened to is violated. Thompson argued that if there is such a thing as the right to privacy it is essentially part of a cluster of other rights over person and property (Thompson, 1975). Developing this argument Reiman suggested that the right to privacy exists independently of other rights and that it protects the individual's interest in becoming, being and remaining a person: 'Personal and property rights pre-suppose an individual with title to his existence – and privacy is the social ritual by which that title is confirmed' (Reiman, 1976, 43). Similarly, it is argued, when two individuals become a couple, the right of the couple to privacy reflects the independent existence of their relationship. The problem with this argument is that it does not recognise that protection of the couple's right to privacy may be at the expense of other rights accruing to one or the other partner, such as the wife's right to the protection of the law.

Laslett has suggested that structural and normative support for the privacy of the family is a key characteristic of twentieth-century society. In this context she defines privacy as 'structural mechanisms which prohibit or permit observability in the enactment of family roles' (Laslett, 1973, 481). She goes on to argue that an increase in privacy leads to a weakening in social control over what takes place within the family. It is important to see the implications of this change in terms of power. Reducing the power of outsiders to control what goes on within the family can have the effect of increasing the significance of power differentials within the family. As Borkowski, Murch and Walker conclude, 'The irony is that privacy contributes to, and reinforces, the intimacy and sense of solidarity in family life that society values, while it also nurtures and protects the very conditions in which conflict and violence develop' (Borkowski, Murch and Walker, 1983, 113).

Respect for privacy has many implications. On the one hand it can have the effect of protecting ordinary people against the intrusions of the state, of allowing an area of personal autonomy within the imperatives of capitalism, and of providing, at least within the home, a haven in a heartless world. On the other hand, the protection of privacy can allow, within the space defined as private, the exploitation of the weaker by the stronger. In the privacy of the home women can be assaulted by men, children by their parents, the frail elderly by their sons and daughters. The strong can extract valuable resources from the weaker, in the form of time, money and labour, without fear of intervention by outsiders.

The importance of respect for privacy has been formalised in many of the recent documents on human rights, very often in a way that associates privacy with family life and the home. Thus Article 8 of the European Convention on Human Rights reads:

(1) Everyone has the right to respect for his private and family life, his home and his correspondence.
(2) There shall be no interference by a public authority with the exercise of this right except such as is in accordance with the law and is necessary in a democratic society in the interests of national security, public safety or the economic well-being of the country, for the prevention of disorder or crime, for the protection of health or morals, or for the protection of the rights and freedoms of others.
(Quoted and discussed in Velu, 1973, 13)

The fact that it is *his* and not *her* privacy that is to be respected cannot be without significance and influence. Despite the caveats set out in section (2) of Article 8, there is no doubt that, in the minds of many of those who are in a position to infringe the right to privacy, it is indeed the 'head' of the household's privacy that is to be respected. If he refuses entry to a policeman, a social worker or a health visitor, it is his right to privacy that is respected, despite his wife's appeals for help. In many instances, the Englishman's home is indeed still 'his' castle. Efforts to establish that certain aspects of family relations are outside the domain of public authority can strengthen the rights of some individuals at the expense of others (Wexler, 1982).

The definition of what is meant by the private sphere varies both over time and cross-culturally. Westin discussed the ways in which patterns of privacy vary between nations. He saw Britain as characterised by a high degree of personal privacy within the home and of reserve between individuals, coupled with deference towards a ruling class that claims major areas of privacy to protect government operations (Westin, 1970). It is, thus, a society which has a relatively high degree of respect for privacy, or at least for the privacy of certain individuals in certain social situations.

The distinction between private and public spheres is, however, not fixed but can be challenged, redefined and altered over time. As Siltanen and Stanworth suggest, 'the relation of public to private is itself a political issue' (Siltanen and Stanworth, 1984, 186). This book can be seen as a small part of the continuing process of questioning and redefining what we mean by the private sphere. For too long it has been assumed that the private is somehow outside the political arena and that areas of life defined as private are not appropriately placed on public agendas for public discussion. This assumption has been maintained partly by what O'Brien calls the 'phoney wall' between public and private (O'Brien, 1981). Over the last few years, however, there has been a growing interest in the social processes by which so many human activities are relegated to a space defined as private and to the margins of public debate. This interest is summed up in the phrase, 'the personal is political.' Thus recent work on rape, incest, sexual harassment and wife abuse has insisted that these be seen, not as private and personal troubles, but as public issues whose roots lie in the fundamental social and economic structures of society. Insisting that family life is private and therefore completely outside the province of legitimate political intervention can have the effect of leaving the weaker members of families with no defence against the stronger members.

Notes on contributors

Val Binney has been active in Women's Aid groups for five years. She was a member of the research team for the Women's Aid Federation/Department of the Environment project on housing for battered women. She has taught with the Cambridge Women's Studies Collective and is completing research on parent-child relationships. She has recently trained as a clinical psychologist.

Rebecca E. and Russell P. Dobash are both tenured faculty at the University of Stirling, Scotland. Since 1974 they have worked closely with the National Women's Aid Federation (England and Wales) and the Scottish Women's Aid Federation. They have published numerous papers on domestic violence, as well as their highly influential book *Violence Against Wives* (Free Press, 1979). They have served as consultants for the British Department of the Environment and for the US Department of Health, Education and Welfare. They have also been involved in an SSRC French-Anglo exchange focusing on violence against women. They are currently preparing a cross-cultural study on the battered women's movement in the United States and Great Britain called *Women, Violence and the State*, to be published by Routledge & Kegan Paul.

Katherine Cavanagh is a graduate of Stirling University and trained as a social worker at Warwick University. From 1975 to 1978 she was a research assistant on the Dobashes' project on violence against wives. Currently she is a social worker with the Leicestershire County Council where she continues to be involved, from a feminist perspective, in areas of wife assault and child abuse.

Tony Faragher graduated from Brunel University in 1971 in sociology, psychology and economics. After working as a researcher with the Wiltshire Social Services Department he moved to take up a three-year DHSS-funded Research Fellowship with the Battered Women's Project at the University of Keele. After two years spent looking after his youngest child, he is currently working for NACRO in a community development role on disadvantaged housing estates.

Gina Harkell graduated in economic and social history and politics at the University of Kent and then did an MA in social history at the University of Essex. She helped to set up Canterbury Women's Aid and worked with Colchester Women's Aid. She was a researcher on the Women's Aid Federation project. Her publications include work on Edwardian women as well as the Women's Aid Federation publication, *Leaving Violent Men*. She has also worked professionally as a jazz singer.

Mary Maynard is a lecturer in sociology at the University of York, where she has tried to promote courses on women, particularly from a feminist perspective. In addition to her work on domestic violence, she is primarily concerned with the development of feminist theories. She is currently writing a jointly authored book on racial and sexual oppression.

Judy Nixon was a founder member of York Women's Aid. She was involved in the refuge movement for four years and worked in several refuges before joining the Women's Aid Federation research team in 1977. She is at present working in the Housing Department of Sheffield City Council.

Jan Pahl is a Research Fellow at the University of Kent at Canterbury. She is attached to the Health Services Research Unit and teaches for the Board of Studies in Social Policy and Administration. Completed research includes work on the links between employment patterns and family life, as well as the study of battered women and women's refuges described in this book. She is now working on an SSRC-funded project on the allocation of money within the family and is directing an evaluative study of community services for mentally handicapped children.

Stephen Parker is a solicitor and lecturer in Law at University College, Cardiff. He has written a number of articles on family law and a textbook on the legal position of unmarried cohabitees.

Bibliography

Amsden, A. (1980), *The Economics of Women and Work*, Harmondsworth, Penguin Books.

Angel, R.C. (1936), *The Family Encounters the Depression*, New York, Scrivener.

Ansell, J. (1978), *A Charter of Protection: A Pilot Study of the Working of the Domestic Violence and Matrimonial Proceedings Act*, London, Women's Aid Federation (England).

Bakke, E.W. (1933), *The Unemployed Man*, London, Nisbet.

Barr, N.A. and Carrier, J. (1978), 'Women's Aid groups: the economic case for state assistance to battered wives', *Policy and Politics*, vol. 6, no. 6, pp. 333-50.

Barrett, M. and McIntosh, M. (1982), *The Anti-social Family*, London, Verso Editions.

Barron, R.D. and Norris, G.M. (1976), 'Sexual divisions and the dual labour market', in D. Leonard Barker and S. Allen, *Dependence and Exploitation in Work and Marriage*, London, Longmans.

Beechey, V. (1979), 'On patriarchy', *Feminist Review*, vol. 1, no. 3, pp. 66-82.

Berk, S.F. and Loseke, D. (1981), ' "Handling" family violence: situational determinants of police arrest in domestic disturbance', *Law and Society Review*, vol. 15, no. 2, pp. 317-46.

Bernstein, R.J. (1976), *The Restructuring of Social and Political Theory*, Oxford, Basil Blackwell.

Binney, V. (1981), 'Domestic violence: battered women in Britain in the 1970's', in Cambridge Women's Collective (ed.), *Women in Society*, London, Virago.

Binney, V., Harkell, G. and Nixon, J. (1980a), *Refuge and Housing for Battered Women in England and Wales*. Final report of the

196

Women's Aid Federation/Department of the Environment Research Team.

Binney, V., Harkell, G. and Nixon, J. (1980b), 'The other victims of marital violence', *Community Care*, 7 March.

Binney, V., Harkell, G. and Nixon, J. (1981), *Leaving Violent Men: A Study of Refuges and Housing for Battered Women*, Leeds, Women's Aid Federation (England).

Blackstone, W. (1966), *Commentaries on the Laws of England*, London, Dawsons (first published 1765).

Board of Directors (1976), *Proposal for Home Intervention Team Service: Hamilton-Westworth Region*, Home Intervention Team Project, Hamilton, Ontario, Canada.

Borkowski, M., Murch, M. and Walker, V. (1983), *Marital Violence: The Community Response*, London, Tavistock.

Bowder, B. (1979), 'The wives who ask for it', *Community Care*, 1 March, pp. 18-19.

Bradshaw, J. (1972), 'The concept of social need', *New Society*, 30 March, p. 496.

Brannen, J.A. (1980), 'Seeking help for marital problems: a conceptual approach', *British Journal of Social Work*, vol. 10, no. 4, pp. 457-70.

Breines, W. and Gordon, L. (1983), 'The new scholarship on family violence', *Signs*, vol. 8, no. 3, pp. 490-531.

Brenner, M.H. (1977), 'Health costs and benefits of economic policy', *International Journal of Health Studies*, vol. 7, no. 4.

Brittan, A. (1977), *The Privatised World*, London, Routledge & Kegan Paul.

Brown, G.W. and Harris, T. (1978), *The Social Origins of Depression*, London, Tavistock.

Bruegel, I. (1979), 'Women as a reserve army of labour', *Feminist Review*, vol. 1, no. 3, pp. 12-23.

Cain, M.E. (1973), *Society and the Policeman's Role*, London, Routledge & Kegan Paul.

Cain, M.E. (1977), 'An ironical departure: the dilemma of contemporary policing', in K. Jones, M. Brown and S. Baldwin (eds) *The Yearbook of Social Policy in Britain*, London, Routledge & Kegan Paul.

Cartwright, A. (1967), *Patients and their Doctors*, London, Routledge & Kegan Paul.

Bibliography

Cavanagh, K. (1978), 'Battered women and social control: a study of the help-seeking behaviour of battered women and the help-giving behaviour of those from whom they seek help', unpublished thesis, University of Stirling.'

Cavanagh, K. (1981), 'The child abuse case conference: a feminist analysis', unpublished thesis, Department of Applied Social Studies, University of Warwick.

Central Statistical Office (1979), *Social Trends*, no. 9, London, HMSO.

Central Statistical Office (1983), *Social Trends*, no. 13, London, HMSO.

Chagnon, N. (1968), *Yanamano – The Fierce People*, New York, Holt, Reinhart & Winston.

Chester, R. and Streather, J. (1972), 'Cruelty in English divorce: some empirical findings', *Journal of Marriage and the Family*, vol. 4, no. 4, pp. 706-10.

Colledge, M. (1982), 'Economic cycles and health: towards a sociological understanding of the impact of the recession on health and illness', *Journal of Social Science and Medicine*, vol. 16, no. 22, pp. 1919-28.

Colledge, M. and Bartholomew, R. (1980), 'The long-term unemployed: some new evidence', *Employment Gazette*, January.

Convention of Scottish Local Authorities (1980), *The Funding of Voluntary and Independent Groups Working with Battered Women*, obtainable from COSLA, 3 Forres Street, Edinburgh.

Council for the Education and Training of Health Visitors (1977), *An Investigation into the Principles of Health Visiting*, published by CETHV, Clifton House, Euston Road, London.

Culyer, A. (1976), *Need and the National Health Service*, London, Martin Robertson.

Dahl, T.S. and Snare, A. (1978), 'The coercion of privacy: a feminist perspective', in C. Smart and B. Smart (eds), *Women, Sexuality and Social Control*, London, Routledge & Kegan Paul.

Davidoff, L., L'Esperance, J. and Newby, H. (1976), 'Landscape with figures', in J. Mitchell and A. Oakley (eds), *The Rights and Wrongs of Women*, Harmondsworth, Penguin Books.

Davis, G. and Murch, M. (1977), 'Implications of special procedure in divorce', *Family Law*, vol. 7, no. 3, pp. 71-8.

Dawson, B. and Faragher, T. (1977), *Battered Women's Project: Interim Report*, Keele, Department of Sociology, University of Keele.

Defoe, D. (1728), 'Augusta Triumphans, or, the way to make London the most flourishing city in the universe', reprinted in L.A. Curtis *The Versatile Defoe*, Totowa, New Jersey, Fowman & Littlefeld, 1979.

Delamont, S. and Ellis, R. (1979), *Statutory and Voluntary Responses to Domestic Violence in Wales*, SRU Working Paper no. 6, Cardiff, Department of Sociology, University College.

Department of the Environment (1978), *Statistics on Homelessness*, unpublished paper.

Dobash, R.E. and Dobash, R.P. (1978), 'Wives: the "appropriate" victims of marital violence', *Victimology*, vol. 2, no. 3-4, pp. 426-42.

Dobash, R.E. and Dobash, R.P. (1979), *Violence Against Wives in Scotland*, Research report for the Scottish Home and Health Department.

Dobash, R.E. and Dobash, R.P. (1980), *Violence Against Wives: A Case Against the Patriarchy*, Shepton Mallet, Open Books.

Dobash, R.E. and Dobash, R.P. (1981a), 'Social science and social action: the case of wife beating', *Journal of Family Issues*, vol. 2, no. 4, pp. 439-70.

Dobash, R.P. and Dobash, R.E. (1981b), 'Community response to violence against wives: charivari, abstract justice and patriarchy', *Social Problems*, vol. 28, no. 5, June, pp. 563-81.

Dobash, R.P. and Dobash, R.E. (1983), 'The context specific approach to researching violence against wives', in G. Hotaling *et al.* (eds), *Issues and Controversies in Studying Family Violence*, Beverly Hills, Sage.

Dobash, R.E., Dobash, R.P., Cavanagh, K. and Wilson, M. (1978), 'Wifebeating: the victims speak', *Victimology*, vol. 2, no. 3-4, pp. 608-922.

Donzelot, J. (1980), *The Policing of Families*, New York, Pantheon.

Eekelaar, J.M. (1971), *Family Security and Family Breakdown*, Harmondsworth, Penguin Books.

Eekelaar, J.M. and Katz, S.N. (1978), *Family Violence*, Toronto, Butterworths.

Elsey, A. (1980), *Battered Women – An Appraisal of Social Policy*, MSc thesis, Cranfield Institute of Technology.

Elshtain, J.B. (1981), *Public Man, Private Woman*, Oxford, Martin Robertson.

Elston, J., Fuller, J. and Murch, M. (1975), 'Judicial hearings of undefended divorce proceedings', *Modern Law Review*, November.

Bibliography

Evason, E. (1980), *Just Me and the Kids*, Equal Opportunities Commission for Northern Ireland.

Evason, E. (1982), *Hidden Violence*, Belfast, Farset Press.

Fagin, L. and Little, M. (1984), *The Forsaken Families*, Harmondsworth, Penguin Books.

Faragher, A. (1980), 'The response of the police to the problem of marital violence', in R. Frankenberg *et al.*, *Battered Women Project*, University of Keele, report to the Department of Health and Social Security.

Faulk, M. (1974), 'Men who assault their wives', *Medicine, Science and the Law*, vol. 7, no. 2, pp. 180-3.

Ferri, E. (1976), *Growing Up in a One Parent Family*, London, National Foundation for Educational Research.

Finch, J. and Groves, D. (1983), *A Labour of Love: Women, Work and Caring*, London, Routledge & Kegan Paul.

Forder, A. (1974), *Concepts in Social Administration*, London, Routledge & Kegan Paul.

Frankenberg, R., Johnson, N., Dawson, B. and Faragher, T. (1980), *Battered Women's Project*, University of Keele, report presented to the Department of Health and Social Security.

Freeman, M. (1979), *Violence in the Home*, Farnborough, Saxon House.

Freeman, M.D.A. (1980), 'Violence against women: does the legal system provide solutions or itself constitute the problem?', *British Journal of Law and Society*, vol. 7, pp. 215-41.

Gaguin, D.A. (1978), 'Spouse abuse: data from the national crime survey', *Victimology*, vol. 2, nos 3-4, pp. 632-43.

Gamarnikow, E., Morgan, D., Purvis, D. and Taylorson, D. (1983), *The Public and the Private*, London, Heinemann.

Gayford, J.J. (1975), 'Wife battering: a preliminary survey of 100 cases', *British Medical Journal*, vol. 1, pp. 194-7.

Gayford, J.J. (1976), 'Ten types of battered wives', *The Welfare Officer*, no. 1, pp. 5-9.

Gelles, R. (1979), 'Violence in the American Family', in J. Martin (ed.), *Violence and the Family*, Chichester, Wiley.

Gelles, R.J. (1974), *The Violent Home*, Beverly Hills, Sage.

Gelles, R.J. (1979), 'Abused wives: why do they stay?', in R. Gelles (ed.), *Family Violence*, Beverly Hills, Sage.

George, V. and Wilding, P. (1972), *Motherless Families*, London, Routledge & Kegan Paul.

Giordano, P. (1977), 'The client's perspective in agency evaluation', *Social Work*, January, pp. 34-7.

Glastonbury, P., Burdett, H. and Austen, R. (1973), 'Community perceptions and the personal social services', *Policy and Politics*, vol. 1, no. 3, pp. 191-211.

Gouldner, A.W. (1975), 'The sociologist as partisan: sociology and the welfare state', in *For Sociology: Research and Critique in Sociology Today*, Harmondsworth, Penguin Books.

Gouldner, A.W. (1976), *The Dialectics of Ideology and Technology*, London, Macmillan.

Greenley, J.R. and Mechanic, D. (1976), 'Social selection in seeking help for psychological problems', *Journal of Health and Social Behaviour*, vol. 17, September, pp. 249-62.

Hagemann-White, C. (1981), *Hilfen fur mishandelte Frauen*, Stuttgart, Verlag W. Kohlhammer.

Hall, S. (1977), 'Culture, the media and the "ideological effect" ', in J. Curran et al. (eds), *Mass Communication and Society*, London, Open University Press.

Hall, S., Critcher, C., Jefferson, T., Clarke, J.and Roberts, B. (1978), *Policing the Crisis: Mugging, the State and Law and Order*, London, Macmillan.

Hanmer, J. (1978), 'Violence and the social control of women', in G. Littlejohn (ed.), *Power and the State*, London, Croom Helm.

Hanmer, J. (1983), 'Blowing the cover of the protective male: a community study of violence to women', in E. Gamarnikow, D. Morgan, J. Purvis and D. Taylorson (eds), *The Public and the Private*, London, Heinemann.

Hanmer, J. and Leonard, D. (1984), 'Negotiating the problem: the DHSS and research on violence in marriage', in C. Bell and H. Roberts (eds), *Social Researching*, London, Routledge & Kegan Paul.

Hilberman, E. and Munson, K. (1978), 'Sixty battered women', *Victimology*, vol. 2, no. 3-4, pp.460-70.

Hill, J.M. (1978), 'The psychological impact of unemployment', *New Society*, 19 January, pp. 118-20.

Homer, M., Leonard, P. and Taylor, P. (1984), *Private Violence and Public Shame*, Cleveland Refuge and Aid for Women and Children.

Houghton, H. (1973), *Separated Wives and Supplementary Benefit*, DHSS, Social Research Branch.

Imray, L. and Middleton, A. (1983), 'Public and private: marking the boundaries', in E. Gamarnikow, D. Morgan, J.Purvis and D. Taylorson (eds), *The Public and the Private*, London, Heinemann.

Bibliography

Jahoda, M., et al., (1972), *Marienthal: the Sociography of an Unemployed Community*, London, Tavistock (first published 1933).

Kenny, D. and Thompson, J.Q. (1978), *Refuges for Battered Women in London – Provision and Need*, Greater London Council.

Kidd, T. (1982), 'Social security and the family', in I. Reid and E. Wormald (eds), *Sex Differences in Britain*, London, Grant McIntyre.

Komarovsky, M. (1940), *The Unemployed Man and his Family*, New York, Octagon Books.

Lamb, R.W. (1983), 'Wife beaters to be arrested', *The Times*, 18 April.

Land, H. (1969), *Large Families in London*, London, Bell.

Laslett, B. (1973), 'The family as a public and private institution – an historical perspective', *Journal of Marriage and the Family*, vol. 35, August, pp. 480-92.

Law Commission (1982), *No. 115, The Implications of Williams and Glyn's Bank v. Boland*, Cmnd. 8836, London, HMSO.

Leonard, P. and McLeod, E. (1980), *Marital Violence: Social Construction and Social Service Response*, Warwick, Department of Applied Social Studies, University of Warwick.

Levinger, G. (1960), 'Continuance in casework and other helping relationships: a review of current research, *Social Work*, vol. 5, no. 3, pp. 40-51.

Loizos, P. (1978), 'Violence and the family: some Mediterranean examples', in J. Martin (ed.), *Violence in the Family*, Chichester, Wiley.

McCabe, S. and Sutcliffe, F. (1978), *Defining Crime*, Oxford, Basil Blackwell.

McCann, K. (1981), 'The relevance of magistrates' domestic jurisdiction to wife abuse', paper presented to the Department of Health and Social Security Seminar on Violence in the Family, University of Kent at Canterbury.

McClintock, E.H. (1963), *Causes of Violence*, New York, St. Martin's Press.

McIntosh, M. (1978), 'The state and the oppression of women', in A. Kuhn and A.M. Wolpe (eds), *Feminism and Materialism*, London, Routledge & Kegan Paul.

Marris, P. (1958), *Widows and their Families*, London, Routledge & Kegan Paul.

Marsden, D. (1973), *Mothers Alone*, Harmondsworth, Penguin Books.

Marsden, D. (1978), 'Sociological perspectives on family violence', in J. Martin (ed.), *Violence and the Family*, Chichester, Wiley.

Martin, D. (1976), *Battered Wives*, San Francisco, Glide Publications.

Martin, J. (1978), *Violence and the Family*, Chichester, Wiley.

May, M. (1978), 'Violence in the family: an historical perspective', in J. Martin (ed.), *Violence and the Family*, Chichester, Wiley.

Mayer, J.E. and Timms, N. (1970), *The Client Speaks*, London, Routledge & Kegan Paul.

Migdall, S.D. (1980), 'Domestic violence – has the act beaten it?', *Family Law*, vol. 9, no. 5, p. 136.

Mill, J.S. (1912), *The Subjection of Women*, reprinted by Oxford University Press.

Mueller, J.H., Schussler, K.F. and Costner, H.L. (1970), *Statistical Reasoning in Sociology*, Boston, Houghton Mifflin.

Murch, M. (1981), *Community Response to Marital Violence*, Bristol, Department of Social Administration, Bristol University. Report presented to the Department of Health and Social Security.

Nichols, B.B. (1976), 'The abused wife problem', *Social Casework*, vol. 57, January, pp. 27-32.

Oakley, A. (1974), *The Sociology of Housework*, Oxford, Martin Robertson.

O'Brien, M. (1981), *The Politics of Reproduction*, London, Routledge & Kegan Paul.

Owen, G.M. (1977), *Health Visiting*, Philadelphia, Baillière Tindall.

Pagelow, M. (1981), *Woman-battering: Victims and their Experiences*, Beverley Hills, Sage.

Pahl, J. (1978), *A Refuge for Battered Women*, London, HMSO.

Pahl, J. (1979a), 'Refuges for battered women: social provision or social movement?', *Journal of Voluntary Action Research*, vol. 8, nos. 1-2, pp. 25-35.

Pahl, J. (1979b), 'The general practitioner and the problems of battered women', *Journal of Medical Ethics*, vol. 5, no. 3, pp. 117-23.

Pahl, J. (1980), 'Patterns of money management within marriage', *Journal of Social Policy*, vol. 9, no. 3, pp. 313-35.

Bibliography

Pahl, J. (1981), *A Bridge Over Troubled Waters: A Longitudinal Study of Women Who Went to a Refuge.* Report presented to the Department of Health and Social Security.

Pahl, J. (1982a), 'Police response to battered women', *Journal of Social Welfare Law*, November, pp. 337-43.

Pahl, J. (1982b), 'Men who assault their wives: what can health visitors do to help?', *Health Visitor*, vol. 55, pp. 528-30.

Pahl, J. (1983), 'The allocation of money and the structuring of inequality within marriage', *Sociological Review*, vol. 31, no. 2.

Pahl, J. (1985), 'Refuges for battered women: women's liberation in action', *Feminist Review*, 19.

Parker, S.J. (1981), *Cohabitees*, Chichester, Barry Rose.

Parnas, R. (1967), 'Police response to the domestic disturbance', *Wisconsin Law Review*, Fall, pp. 914-60.

Parry, M.L. (1981), *Cohabitation*, London, Sweet & Maxwell.

Pfouts, J.H. (1978), 'Violent families: coping responses of abused wives', *Child Welfare*, vol. LVII, no. 2, pp. 101-11.

Pizzey, E. (1974), *Scream Quietly or the Neighbours Will Hear*, Harmondsworth, Penguin Books.

Pizzey, E. and Shapiro, J. (1982), *Prone to Violence*, Feltham, Middlesex, Hamlyn.

Popay, J. (1981), *Unemployment: A Threat to Public Health*, London, Child Poverty Action Group.

Popay, J., Rimmer, L. and Rossiter, C. (1983), *One Parent Families: Parents, Children and Public Policy*, London, Study Commission on the Family.

Rees, S. (1974), 'No more than contact: an outcome of social work', *British Journal of Social Work*, vol. 4, no. 3, pp. 255-79.

Rees, S. (1978), *Social Work Face to Face*, London, Edward Arnold.

Reiner, R. (1978), *The Blue-coated Worker*, Cambridge University Press.

Reiman, J. (1976), 'Privacy, intimacy and personhood', *Philosophy and Public Affairs*, vol. 6, pp. 26-44.

Reiss, A.J. (1971), 'Systematic observation of natural social phenomena', in H.L. Costner (ed.), *Sociological Methodology*, San Francisco, Jossey-Bass.

Reith, D. (1975), 'I wonder if you can help me', *Social Work Today*, vol. 6, no. 3, pp. 66-9.

Report of the Actuaries in Relation to the Proposed Scheme of Insurance against Sickness (1910), 21 March, 51.

Report of the Committee on One Parent Families (1974), *Finer Report*, Cmnd. 5629, London, HMSO.

Report of the Committee on Privacy (1972), *Younger Report*, Cmnd. 5012, London, HMSO.

Rights of Women (1981), *The Cohabitation Handbook*, London, Pluto Press.

Roldan, M. (1982), *Patterns of Money Allocation and Women's Subordination*, unpublished paper.

Rosaldo, M.Z. and Lamphere, L. (1974), *Woman, Culture and Society*, Stamford, Conn., Stamford University Press.

Rounsaville, B.J. (1977), 'Battered wives: barriers to identification and treatment', *American Journal of Orthopsychiatry*, vol. 48, no. 3, pp. 487-95.

Rounsaville, B. and Weissman, M.M. (1977-8), 'Battered women: a medical problem requiring detection', *International Journal of Psychiatry in Medicine*, vol. 8, no. 2, pp. 191-202.

Roy, M. (1977), *Battered Women: a psycho-sociological study of Domestic Violence*, London, Van Nostrand Reinhold.

Ryan, W. (1971), *Blaming the Victim*, New York, Random House.

Sainsbury, E. (1975), *Social Work with Families*, London, Routledge & Kegan Paul.

Saunders, S. (1982), *A Study of Domestic Violence: Battered Women in Israel*, London, Anglo-Israel Association.

Schecter, S. (1978), 'Wife battering: the institutional response to battered women', paper presented at the Midwest Conference on Abuse of Women, St. Louis, May.

Schlegel, A. (1972), *Male Dominance and Female Autonomy: Domestic Authority in Matrilineal Societies*, New Haven, Hraf Press.

Scott, P.D. (1974), 'Battered wives', *British Journal of Psychiatry*, no. 125, pp. 433-41.

Scottish Women's Aid (1980), *Local Group Reports and Statistics*, 11 Colme Street, Edinburgh, Scottish Women's Aid.

Select Committee Report (1975), *Violence in Marriage*, HCP, 553, II.

Sennett, R. (1974), *The Fall of Public Man*, Cambridge University Press.

Bibliography

Service Delivery Assessment (1980), *Domestic Violence*, report for the Department of Health, Education and Welfare, Washington, DC.

Shainess, N. (1977), 'Psychological aspects of wife beating', in M. Roy (ed.), *Battered Women: A Psychological Study of Violence*, New York, Van Nostrand Reinhold.

Shaw, J. (1974), *The Self in Social Work*, London, Routledge & Kegan Paul.

Sherman, L.W. and Berk, R.A. (1984), 'The specific deterrent effects of arrest for domestic assault', *American Sociological Review*, vol. 49, no. 2, pp. 261-72.

Showler, B. and Sinfield, A. (1981), *The Workless State*, Oxford, Martin Robertson.

Siltanen, J. and Stanworth, M. (1984), 'The politics of public man and private woman', in J. Siltanen and M. Stanworth (eds), *Women and the Public Sphere*, London, Hutchinson.

Skolnick, J.H. (1967), *Justice without Trial*, New York, Wiley.

Snell, J.E., Rosenwald, R.J. and Robey, A. (1964), 'The wife-beater's wife', *Archives of General Psychiatry*, vol. 11, August, pp. 107-12.

Stark, E., Flitcraft, A. and Frazier, W. (1979), 'Medicine and patriarchial violence, *International Journal of Health Services*, vol. 9, no. 3, pp. 461-93.

Stark, E., Flitcraft, A., Zuckerman, D., Grey, A. and Frazier, W. (1979), 'Domestic violence and female suicide attempts', paper presented to the American Public Health Association.

Storr, A. (1974), *Human Aggression*, Harmondsworth, Penguin Books.

Straus, M. (1978), 'Wife beating: how common and why', in J. Eekelar and S. Katz (eds), *Family Violence*, Toronto, Butterworths.

Straus, M., Gelles, R.J. and Steinmetz, S.K. (1980), *Behind Closed Doors: Violence in the American Family*, New York, Anchor Books.

Study Commission on the Family (1983), *Families in the Future*, London, Final Report of the Study Commission on the Family.

Sutton, J. (1979), 'Modern and Victorian battered women', in *Battered Women and Abused Children*, Occasional Paper no. 4, University of Bradford.

Thompson, J.J. (1975), 'The right to privacy', *Philosophy and Public Affairs*, vol. 4, no. 4, pp. 295-314.

Tomes, N. (1978), 'A torrent of abuse: causes of violence between working class men and women in London 1840-1975', *Journal of Social History*, vol. 11, no. 3, pp. 329-45.

Velu, J. (1973), 'The European Convention on Human Rights and the right to respect for private life, the home and communications', in A.H. Robertson (ed.), *Privacy and Human Rights*, Manchester University Press.

Wasoff, F. (1982), 'Legal protection from wife beating: the processing of domestic assaults by Scottish prosecutors and criminal courts', *International Journal of Sociology of Law*, vol. 10, pp. 187-204.

Weiss, R. (1973), 'Helping relationships: relations of clients with physicians, social workers, priests and others', *Social Problems*, vol. 20, no. 3, pp. 319-28.

Welsh Women's Aid (1980a), *Mrs. Hobson's Choice: A Survey of the Employment Position of Women who have been through Women's Aid Refuges in South Wales*, Cardiff, Welsh Women's Aid.

Welsh Women's Aid (1980b), *Which Venue Now?*, Incentive House, Adam Street, Cardiff.

Westin, A. (1970), *Privacy and Freedom*, London, Bodley Head.

Wexler, S. (1982), 'Battered women and public policy', in E. Boneparth (ed.), *Women, Power and Policy*, New York, Pergamon Press.

Wilson, E. (1975), 'A social worker's view point', *Royal Society of Health Journal*, vol. 95, no. 6, pp. 294-7.

Wilson, E. (1977), *Women and the Welfare State*, London, Tavistock.

Wilson, E. (1983), *What is to be Done about Violence against Women?*, Harmondsworth, Penguin Books.

Wilson, J.Q. (1968), *Varieties of Police Behaviour*, Cambridge, Mass., Harvard University Press.

Women's Aid Federation (England) (1980a), *Annual Report 1979-80*, London, Women's Aid Federation (England).

Women's Aid Federation (England) (1980b), 'An abnormal number of malevolent doorknobs: battered women and the medical profession, a preliminary survey', London, Women's Aid Federation, 52-54 Featherstone Street, London, EC1Y 8RY.

Women's Aid Federation (England) Research Group (1981), 'Violence to Women in the home: a research strategy', paper presented to the Department of Health and Social Security seminar on Violence in the Family at the University of Kent.

Young, J.B. (1978), *Privacy*, Chichester, Wiley.

Zaretsky, E. (1976), *Capitalism, the Family and Personal Life*, London, Pluto Press.

Index

Index